You Can Profit
from the
New Tax Law

YOU CAN PROFIT
from the
NEW TAX LAW

Joseph L. Wiltsee

Attorney and Associate Editor,
Business Week

and

Donna Sammons

Financial Writer and Correspondent,
McGraw-Hill World News

MCGRAW-HILL BOOK COMPANY

New York St. Louis San Francisco Auckland Bogotá Guatemala Hamburg
Johannesburg Lisbon London Madrid Mexico Montreal New Delhi Panama
Paris San Juan São Paulo Singapore Sydney Tokyo Toronto

1 2 3 4 5 6 7 8 9 F G F G 8 7 6 5 4 3 2

ISBN 0-07-070963-7

LIBRARY OF CONGRESS CATALOGING IN PUBLICATION DATA

Wiltsee, Joseph L.
  You can profit from the new tax law.

  Includes index.
  1. Income tax—United States. I. Sammons, Donna.
II. Title
HJ4652.W66

	343.7305'2	81-20844
ISBN 0-07-070963-7 (pbk.)	347.30352	AACR2

Book design by Roberta Rezk

Contents

You Can Profit
from the
New Tax Law

Chapter 1 _____

Overview of the New Tax Law

Its authors call it the Economic Recovery Tax Act of 1981, a name that suggests a legislative package of historic proportions. Is it? Numbers of accounting firms and tax lawyers think so and point out that it is the largest single rewrite of the United States Tax Code since 1954. They also say it is the most significant reduction ever in the amount of money the United States collects from its citizens—an estimated $2 billion cut from revenues in 1981 and expanding to a reduction of $150 billion in 1984.

But will it accomplish its principal goal? Will it stimulate true economic recovery? Neither President Reagan's advisors nor Wall Street's economists are sure, although both groups agree that the tax act will move the country closer to the practice of "supply-side economics." How? The Economic Recovery Tax Act sets a federal tax policy that encourages both saving and investing. Additionally, it reaffirms federal tax policies that seek not to redistribute the country's wealth among all citizens but to correct certain economic disincentives.

What this means to individual American taxpayers is this:

• You will be taking home more of the money you earn, and

• You will be provided with a number of new tax breaks to further reduce your annual tax burden.

That first item is a "giveaway." You need do nothing to take advantage of it. Your employer will do it for you, reducing the amount of money you pay to the Internal Revenue Service through payroll deductions. These scheduled increases in take-home pay will occur as the withholding tax rates are reduced under the law—first by 5 percent in late 1981 (a gain you have already realized), then by 10 percent in 1982, and finally by another 10 percent in 1983. Further reductions in the tax rates will be put into place beginning in 1985 when "indexing"—a system decreasing taxes as the cost of living rises—is instituted.

Profiting from this part of the new tax law is easy. What is more difficult is capturing the other breaks outlined by the new law so that you may further reduce your overall tax load. This requires that you do some tax planning or pay someone to do it for you. Tax accountants will charge from $40 to $60 an hour in most places except major cities, where they often charge $100 or more an hour. You may find their help worthwhile, especially if you are a high-bracket taxpayer and your tax affairs are complicated.

Whether or not you need help in managing your tax affairs is a decision you must make and make carefully. But regardless of that decision, it is important that you understand the basic provisions of the new tax law. Just as you would not turn over the management of all your finances without retaining certain controls and certain decision-making responsibilities, you should not blindly allow someone else to be totally in charge of your taxpaying obligations. Know how the tax system works. It is in your best interest.

The Economic Recovery Tax Act of 1981, adopted by Congress on August 4, 1981, and signed into law by President Reagan a little more than a week later, provides benefits, both small and large, for everyone—benefits anyone who files a federal tax return would be foolish to shrug off. It also is a moneyed person's tax bill, as has been widely discussed, because these benefits occur primarily in the legislation's treatment of investments and in its creation of new tax loopholes.

The basic provisions of the bill are these:

• *A Tax Cut*. Under prior law, Americans paid from 14 percent to 50 percent of their "personal service income," meaning wages, salaries, and bonuses, to the federal government in taxes. Also, they forwarded to the Internal Revenue Service as much as 70 percent of their "unearned income," which is the amount of money received from investments: interest payments, royalties, rents, and so on. The new law reduces the top rate of taxation to 50 percent on *all* income, eliminating the distinction between personal service income and unearned income. This means an immediate, sharp tax reduction for certain high-income citizens. For those of us not in a financial position to benefit from this cut, there is the reduction in the overall tax rates. This cut will total 23 percent by 1984. (A detailed discussion of the impact of the new tax law on your earnings is found in chapter 2.)

• *The Move to Indexing*. The Economic Recovery Tax Act orders the Treasury Department to institute a system of indexing in 1985. This means that the tax rates and subsequently the tax tables will be adjusted downward annually for inflation. Inflation will be measured using the Consumer Price Index, or CPI as it is commonly called. No one is sure how this system actually will work, although it is hoped that it will help eliminate "bracket creep"—the name for the bind we find ourselves in when, after being granted cost-of-living wage increases, we climb into higher tax brackets.

• *Incentives for Saving*. In an effort to revitalize the nation's sagging savings institutions, the Economic Recovery Tax Act has created a new saving device, the all-savers certificate. This vehicle permits taxpayers to earn up to $1,000 in interest tax-free during 1982 ($2,000 tax-free for a couple filing a joint return). The appeal of these certificates depends upon your tax bracket. Specifically, higher-income persons will gain more from depositing their money in all-savers certificates than those of lesser means. (To determine if all-savers certificates are a wise investment for you, turn to chapter 4.)

• *New Retirement Rules*. The stepped-up IRA is one of the major boons contained within the Economic Recovery Tax Act. It allows each employed person, regardless of whether or not he or she is covered at work by a pension plan, to establish an Individual Retirement Account (IRA), deposit up to $2,000 annually, and to deduct the amount deposited from his or her taxable income. The money grows, tax-free, until the individual reaches retirement age and begins withdrawing it. A "spousal" Individual Retirement Account, meaning one in the name of an employed person and his or her spouse, is permitted, too. The total maximum allowable annual contribution to such accounts where the spouse is nonworking is $2,250; where the spouse is working, the maximum total contribution is $4,000. Self-employed people benefit under the new tax law, as well. Their self-financed retirement accounts, known as Keogh plans, now have a new maximum annual contribution level—$15,000 compared to the previous top rate of $7,500. The rules regarding retirement accounts are complex, and a number of penalties are in place for persons who withdraw these funds early. It is best to understand the regulations prior to establishing an account. (An explanation of the effect of the new tax law on retirement and retirement planning may be found in chapter 6.)

• *Partial Elimination of the Marriage Penalty*. The marriage penalty is the term used to describe the way the tax system discriminates against married persons—the method of discrimination being higher tax rates. For example, two employed people who are married pay more in taxes than two single persons who live together and earn the same total income (and file separate tax returns). The Economic Recovery Tax Act provides for the partial elimination of the marriage penalty by establishing a special tax deduction for working couples. The deduction (maximum $1,500 in 1982 and $3,000 beginning in 1983) is subtracted from your taxable income. The amount of the deduction you may take is based upon your earnings. (Chapter 3 explains how.)

• *Breaks for Workers with Children or Adult Dependents*. The new tax law recognizes that the cost of having someone provide care for your children or incapacitated adults in your household is often a necessary expense: You need help at home so that you are free to go to work. The law increases the allowable tax credits for child and dependent adult care. The new ceilings of these tax credits are $2,400 yearly for one dependent and $4,800 for two or more. (Details are found in chapter 3.)

• *Liberalization of Charitable Contribution Deductions*. The new law allows you to deduct contributions even if you do not formally itemize deductions in filing your tax return. You can file a short-form 1040 and still have the advantage of taking a deduction for your gifts to charity. This is a big change in the law, particularly for many young marrieds who take the standard deduction and do not itemize. (Some ins and outs are explained in chapter 3.)

• *Relaxation of Real Estate Rules*. If you are 55 years of age or older and sell your principal residence, you may pocket a gain on the sale of up to $125,000 and pay no taxes on it. Prior law allowed a similar transaction but limited the tax-free profit to a maximum of $100,000. (An important note: This is a one-time-only offer. You may not sell your principal residence when you are 56, keep the $125,000 profit, then repeat the move 10 years later.) In addition to this break, the new tax law allows you to sell your home—regardless of your age—and pay no taxes on the amount you gain if you reinvest that money in another principal residence within 24 months of the sale. The previous time restriction for reinvestment of such money was 18 months. This rule applies to houses sold after July 20, 1981. (Chapter 5 provides a detailed discussion of the new rules.)

• *Reduction in the Capital Gains Tax Rate*. The capital gains tax, which is the tax levied on profits from the sale of property or investments (real estate and stocks are examples) held for more than one year, is directly tied to the overall rate of taxation. This means that the capital gains rate varies from individual to individual, depending upon his tax bracket. The capital gains rate is computed by multiplying 40 percent by your gain by your tax rate. With the reduction of the top tax rate from 70 percent to 50 percent, the capital gains tax drops from a ceiling of 28 percent to 20 percent. Your capital gains tax rate will be even less if you are in a tax bracket below 50 percent. (Chapter 8 describes the effect of the new tax law.

• *New Pluses for Executives*. The new law establishes a device called an Incentive Stock Option—ISO for short. These options are basically awards granted executives as part of their company fringe-benefit packages. The options give the executives the right to purchase a stated number of shares in their corporation at a stated price. It does not matter what the stock is selling for the day the executive purchases it; he simply pays the amount listed in the stock option. The options are attractive because they are not taxed by the federal government at the time they are issued or at the time they are exercised, meaning when the stock is purchased. Tax is due only when the stock is sold and gain is realized. (Information about these and other advantages for the executive class is found in chapter 7.)

• *Exemptions for Americans Who Live Abroad*. If you are an American taxpayer working abroad, the Economic Recovery Tax Act allows you to exempt up to $75,000 of your earnings from taxation by the United States in 1982. That figure climbs to $95,000 in 1986. This benefit is not as sizable as you may think, since Americans living outside the country are subject to taxation in the nation in which they are residing. Also, most major corporations with employees abroad maintain "tax equalization policies." This means that the company provides net earnings overseas equal to what you would re-receive if you lived and worked in the United States. Who profits from this portion of the law? Mainly companies with equalization policies employing persons in countries having low tax rates—Saudi Arabia, for example. Still, many changes in the law help many expatriate workers. (Chapter 9 describes how.)

• *Estate and Gift Tax Breaks.* The Economic Recovery Tax Act substantially increases the value of estates exempt from taxation. For example, the law says that for 1982 no taxes are to be levied on estates valued up to $225,000. That figure will climb to $600,000 beginning in 1987. The law also establishes a new rule that you can leave all of your estate to your spouse tax-free. (A description of the act as it pertains to estates and gifts may be found in chapter 10.)

The Higher Cost of Making
a Tax-Filing Mistake

Although the Economic Recovery Tax Act provides a variety of tax breaks, it also sets new penalties for those who do not conform. Among these are higher interest rates. Previously, the government imposed a 12 percent interest rate on underpaid taxes. Under the new law, the rate charged will be 20 percent in 1982.

The message here, then, is to be careful, a difficult task given the numbers of changes provided in the new tax law. If you are audited or questioned by the Internal Revenue Service, remember that its agents are generally thorough. Some points to keep in mind:

• Never underestimate the skill of the examining IRS agent. Internal Revenue employees usually are competent, straightforward, and reasonably courteous. They are, how-ever, anxious to secure every tax dollar they think is due the federal government. Your money, in the minds of IRS agents, is their money.

• Never bring more material than is necessary to a tax audit. The typed notice you receive in the mail from the IRS will usually specify what you will need to bring. For example, you may be asked to provide proof of medical deductions, or to furnish receipts listing charitable contributions (a big item now, since the new law lets individuals claim deductions who do not itemize in the usual way). Take with you *only* the receipts or documents listed in the notice, nothing more. To take more is to invite a wider inquiry.

• Do not lean too heavily on a person who prepares your tax return for you. The individual you may hire to prepare your return is responsible only for the way the information is han-dled—not for the information itself. He or she will not be able to defend the accuracy of your paperwork. You must be able to do that. If you find yourself in a serious situation, you may want to consider hiring a tax attorney. An attorney differs from a tax accountant in a variety of ways. Among them: What you tell a lawyer is confidential under the law; conversations with accountants are not protected.

• Never rely on a friend's case or on cases reported in the newspaper. What happened to someone else may not happen to you. The Internal Revenue Service is composed of people, and their approaches are often as varied as their personalities. You may find one agent to be tough, a counterpart more lenient.

• Most audits and partial audits are conducted in the local Internal Revenue Service office. If the IRS invites itself to your home or office for a look at your personal records, as-sume that something is seriously wrong. The advice: Phone a tax accountant or attorney.

You will fare better in an audit situation, of course, if you have a basic understanding of the tax law and how it operates. This will help you not only in your dealings with the IRS but in your tax planning as well—and this is particularly true in view of the huge number of tax changes brought about by the Economic Recovery Tax Act of 1981.

Chapter 2 _____

How the Tax Rate Cuts Work

In general terms, the new tax law reduces individual federal income tax rates by about one-fourth over a 33-month period. The first reduction—5 percent—occurred on October 1, 1981. The second cut—10 percent—takes effect on July 1, 1982, and the third scheduled reduction—another 10 percent—will be put into place on July 1, 1983. This means that on the specified dates the federal withholding tables are reduced by these set-by-law percentages. The prorated tax cut appears in your paycheck as of those dates. Further tax reductions depend on the rate of inflation, since indexing becomes effective as part of the federal system in 1985 (more about this later). The schedule for implementing the tax cuts is illustrated in figure 2–1.

The Economic Recovery Tax Act of 1981 also sets a new reduced maximum tax rate. Previously, a 50 percent ceiling was placed on "personal service income," meaning the wages and bonuses you earn from your job. However, the top tax rate was actually 70 percent, because it was permissible to tax other types of income—dividends, interest, rents, royalties, and so forth—at a higher level. The new tax law reduces the maximum allowable tax rate to 50 percent regardless of the source of income. This is a bonanza for the country's more affluent citizens (see figure 2–1).

FIGURE 2–1

SCHEDULED TAX CUTS

Year	Effective Date	Reduction	Reduces 1980 tax rates by:
1981	10/1/81	5%	1.25%
1982	7/1/82	10	11
1983	7/1/83	10	19
1984	—	—	23

FIGURE 2–2

REDUCTION IN MARGINAL TAX RATES

Taxable Income	Marginal Tax Rates Joint Returns		Single Returns	
	1980	1984	1980	1984
$ 15,000	21%	16%	26%	20%
25,000	32	25	39	30
35,000	37	28	49	38
50,000	49	38	55	42
75,000	54	42	63	48
100,000	59	45	68	50
150,000	64	49	70	50
200,000	68	50	70	50

How Much You Will Save

The later years of the tax cut obviously are the years when the tax savings enable you to invest in something, put more into savings or spend more freely on consumer goods. All these should be a boon both to the economy and to you. Still, the amount of tax savings the new law will produce for you varies with your income, with your marital status and with the total of your deductions.

HOW THE TAX RATE CUTS WORK

To help you determine how much you will save, figures 2–3 through 2–6 are provided. The year-to-year savings figures are calculated assuming annual deductions totaling 23 percent of a taxpayer's income.

FIGURE 2–3

PROJECTED SAVINGS: SINGLE TAXPAYER, NO DEPENDENTS

Income	1981 (3 mo)	1982	1983	1984 (6 mo)	Savings* Total 81–84
$ 15,000	$ 26	$ 212	$ 191	$ 75	$ 504
20,000	39	287	284	113	723
30,000	71	495	545	252	913
40,000	123	831	859	446	2,259
50,000	157	1,082	1,087	650	2,976
100,000	395	927	1,845	1,468	4,635

FIGURE 2–4

PROJECTED SAVINGS: SINGLE PARENT, TWO CHILDREN

(Head of Household)

Income	1981	1982	1983	1984	Savings Total 81–84
$ 15,000	$ 21	$ 169	$ 126	$ 74	$ 390
20,000	30	248	461	564	1,303
30,000	58	418	412	180	1,068
40,000	113	820	816	350	2,099
50,000	135	983	964	424	2,506
100,000	372	1,250	2,349	1,351	5,694

* Savings are down from 1983 and 1984 since percentage tax cuts are based on previously reduced taxes.

Figure 2–5

PROJECTED SAVINGS: MARRIED COUPLE, TWO CHILDREN
(Joint Return)

Income	1981	1982	1983	1984	Savings Total 81–84
$ 15,000	$ 18	$ 152	$ 85	$ 64	$ 319
20,000	25	203	143	93	464
30,000	49	356	339	170	914
40,000	102	737	699	350	1,888
50,000	117	830	807	404	2,158
100,000	348	1,789	2,511	1,174	5,822

Figure 2–6

PROJECTED SAVINGS: MARRIED COUPLE, BOTH WORKING,
NO CHILDREN (Joint Return)

Income	1981	1982	1983	1984	Savings Total 81–84
$ 15,000	$ 18	$ 152	$ 85	$ 64	$ 319
20,000	31	292	23	108	454
30,000	86	503	457	183	1,229
40,000	102	737	699	350	1,888
50,000	127	1,144	1,080	419	2,770
100,000	361	2,408	3,099	1,164	7,032

How Much You Will Pay

The amount you will pay under the new Reagan tax law—
like the amount you save—depends on a variety of factors:
whether you are married, how many dependents you have, the
deductions you accumulate, and so on. Figures 2–7 through

2–10 illustrate total tax liabilities during the next three years for persons in a variety of circumstances—those who are married, those who are single, one-earner households, two-earner couples.

One note: As was the case with the preceding charts, a 23 percent deduction level is assumed in the calculations. If you accumulate deductions in excess of this amount, your tax load will be less than the amount shown. Conversely, deductions below the 23 percent level will result in a tax liability greater than the figure listed.

Figure 2–7

TAXES: SINGLE PERSON, NO DEPENDENTS

Income	1980	1981	1982	1983	1984
$ 15,000	$ 1,555	$ 1,535	$ 1,385	$ 1,257	$ 1,257
20,000	3,115	3,076	2,789	2,505	2,392
30,000	5,718	5,647	5,152	4,637	4,385
40,000	7,434	7,341	6,692	6,045	5,705
50,000	12,559	12,402	11,320	10,233	9,673
100,000	31,792	31,395	30,468	28,623	27,155

Figure 2–8

TAXES: SINGLE PARENT, TWO CHILDREN

(Head of Household)

Income	1980	1981	1982	1983	1984
$ 15,000	$ 1,708	$ 1,687	$ 1,518	$ 1,392	$ 1,318
20,000	2,404	2,374	2,156	1,943	1,840
30,000	4,610	4,552	4,134	3,722	3,543
40,000	6,859	6,773	6,138	5,534	5,290
50,000	10,787	10,652	9,669	8,705	8,281
100,000	29,761	27,530	25,741	23,230	22,056

HOW THE TAX RATE CUTS WORK

Figure 2–9

TAXES: MARRIED COUPLE, TWO CHILDREN   (Joint Return)

Income	1980	1981	1982	1983	1984
$ 15,000	$ 1,404	$ 1,386	$ 1,234	$ 1,149	$ 1,085
20,000	2,013	1,988	1,785	1,642	1,549
30,000	3,917	3,868	3,512	3,173	3,003
40,000	6,201	6,123	5,574	5,034	4,790
50,000	9,323	9,206	8,376	7,569	7,165
100,000	27,878	27,530	25,741	23,230	22,056

Figure 2-10

TAXES: MARRIED COUPLE, NO DEPENDENTS   (Joint Return)

Income	1980	1981	1982	1983	1984
$ 15,000	$ 1,404	$ 1,386	$ 1,234	$ 1,149	$ 1,085
20,000	2,457	2,426	2,134	1,903	1,795
30,000	4,477	4,391	3,918	3,461	3,278
40,000	6,201	6,123	5,574	5,034	4,790
50,000	10,183	10,056	8,912	7,832	7,413
100,000	28,878	28,517	26,109	23,010	21,846

"Bracket Creep"

By reducing overall tax rates and creating a maximum tax of 50 percent on all income, the new tax law addresses the issue of "bracket creep," or "taxflation," as it is sometimes called. Bracket creep occurs when an individual is pushed into a higher tax category by raises in his or her wages, although these increments do not actually represent an increase in real purchasing power or real income. The reason they don't is inflation.

Ironically, many of the raises granted today to workers under labor contracts or paid to white- and blue-collar employees by major corporations actually are cost-of-living ad-

16

justments—increments given to help employees maintain their current financial level, their "standard of living." Yet, the benefits of these cost-of-living raises are seldom felt, because employees—pushed into a higher marginal tax bracket—often pay nearly the total of their increases to the Internal Revenue Service.

For years, the beneficiary of taxflation has been the United States government: The Joint Committee on Taxation estimates that federal individual tax revenues increase at least 16 percent annually, simply because of taxflation. In past years, Congress has tackled the problem by adopting specific legislation to reduce the effects of bracket creep. The last such bill was enacted in 1978.

Following is an example of how bracket creep works:

Jim Porter is forty-two years old, married and works as a middle-level manager for a major utility company. He earns $50,000 annually, and, because of good financial planning, his deductions total $10,000 each year. On April 15, 1981, when he filed his 1980 tax return, it reflected a tax liability of $10,226.

In early 1981, Porter's boss summoned him to his office and announced he was granting him a 12 percent raise. Porter was delighted and made plans to celebrate with an evening out with his wife.

During their $56 dinner, she said she had been wanting a new set of Wedgwood china. He said he had his mind on a set of Bobby Jones golf clubs. Both mentioned the five-speed bicycles their two children had been pleading for.

At the breakfast table the next morning, Porter turned to his wife and said, "What the heck." The two of them then piled into their Ford station wagon, drove to the local department store and purchased the set of china she wanted ($600 for a six-place setting), to the area pro shop to buy the golf clubs he dreamed about ($500), and to the bike shop to procure two shiny European-made bikes ($170 each on sale).

A few weeks later, his paycheck reflecting the salary

increase arrived and reality hit: He and his wife should have dined at Kentucky Fried Chicken. He should have cleaned his aging Wilson clubs; she should have shopped at Sears or a discount store for her new dinnerware; and the kids should still be riding their Schwinns.

The reason:

Porter's 12 percent raise has pushed him from a 43 percent tax bracket into a 49 percent one, meaning his annual tax bill jumped by 25 percent, to $12,800. Out of his $6,000 raise, he will receive—in hand—only 57 percent of it, or $3,400. With inflation running at 12 percent a year, the amount he realizes will not even allow him to remain at his previous year's standard of living. To keep even, Porter needs a salary increase of 17.3 percent, or $8,650.

Porter has become a victim of "bracket creep."

Indexing

Indexing is included in the Reagan tax package as a means of solving bracket creep. Much has been made of indexing, the attempt by the government to erase the damage done to our take-home pay by the combination of ever-higher tax brackets and endless inflation. Canada has tried it, and so have a number of other countries.

How indexing will work for taxpayers in the United States—starting in 1985—is still unclear. But under the Economic Recovery Tax Act, certain specifics are known. These include:

• On December 15, 1984, effective the first day of 1985, tax brackets will be adjusted for changes in the Consumer Price Index occurring between September 30, 1983, and September 30, 1984.

• Each year after that, tax brackets and personal exemptions will be adjusted according to changes in the Consumer Price Index.

• Also affected by changes in the Consumer Price Index will be the "zero bracket amount," the term used for the standard deduction, or personal exemption, as it is sometimes called. It currently stands at $1,000. The new standard deduction will be figured this way: The current amount will be multiplied by the increase in the Consumer Price Index. The product of that will be added to the current standard deduction, and the resulting sum will be the new personal exemption. That is, if the Consumer Price Index increases by 7 percent, the $1,000 personal exemption will increase by 1000 × .07, or $70.

New Rules for Withholding Taxes

Federal law requires our employers to withhold from all of our paychecks a predetermined amount which goes toward satisfying our federal income tax burdens. The amount kept back by our companies and forwarded by them to the Internal Revenue Service is based on tables distributed by the U.S. government. These tables—the withholding tables—list the amount to be retained based on our income and the number of dependents we claim. Our companies know the number of our dependents because we provide them with that figure prior to receiving our first check.

The Internal Revenue Service, recognizing that some of us receive large refunds each year, permits us to claim more personal exemptions than we actually have. (If we list more than nine, though, our employers are required under current law to notify the IRS of that fact.) The problem in doing this—and what has caused the IRS to become suspicious of persons with inflated numbers of dependents—is that it is an often-used method of avoiding paying taxes at the time they are due. (If we all waited until April 15 of one year to pay last year's taxes, the federal government would have no money on which to operate.)

HOW THE TAX RATE CUTS WORK

The difference between a legitimate increase in exemptions for withholding purposes and an illegitimate one is illustrated in the following two examples:

Bob Smith, a Detroit autoworker, squeezed by inflation and anxious over his mounting bills, sees a way to take home more of the money he earns. He informs his company that the number of his dependents has increased from three to ten, and the plant's payroll clerk accepts what Smith says as fact. When he receives his next paycheck, it is fatter—not because of increased earnings but because of a reduction in the amount of federal taxes the company withholds.

Ann Welch is a chemist employed by one of the nation's largest corporations. She invests her small inheritance and her savings in real estate and consequently accumulates large deductions for interest and for maintenance of her rental property. Each year for three years, she receives an income tax refund in excess of $2,000. In early 1982—frustrated because she must forward a large portion of her salary to federal revenue agents only to have them return it to her months later with **no interest earned on it—she decides to alter the number of** personal exemptions she claims. She informs the corporation's payroll department that she is claiming 10 exemptions rather than one, and clerk agrees to make the change. The amount typed on the checks she receives biweekly from the company swells.

Under President Reagan's Economic Recovery Tax Act, Bob Smith may be in trouble. Ann Welch probably is not. The reasons:

• The Economic Recovery Tax Act of 1981 raises the civil penalty from $50 to $500 for employees who provide employers with false information about numbers of exemptions. It **also raises from $500 to $1,000 the criminal penalty for workers** who file fraudulent withholding forms with employers or who fail to furnish the information requested on that form. Bob Smith is subject to these penalties: He falsely reports the number of his dependents. At the end of 1982, he faces a large unpaid federal income tax and penalties, as well. The Internal Revenue Service has reason to be suspect of his intentions.

• While setting penalties, the new tax law continues to grant the U.S. Treasury Department the authority to write regulations to help people adjust the amount withheld from their paychecks to more accurately match their year-end tax liabilities. The idea was and is to enable people to keep more of what they earn at the time they earn it. The idea also was and is to allow employers to alter withholding certificates and subsequently withholding taxes in consideration of an employee's deductions, business losses and tax credits.

This portion of the new law is a boon to Ann Welch: She normally deducts large amounts; she usually receives a tax refund. By claiming 10 exemptions on her withholding certificate, she closes 1982 having paid the federal government about the same amount she owes. She will not be penalized because the amount withheld is near the amount due.

The lesson here is twofold:

• If you do not regularly receive a refund from the IRS, do not claim more than your actual number of exemptions.

• If you usually receive a tax refund, adjust your withholding taxes within the limits of that refund. Do not go to any extremes with this notion—an audit will cost you more than you will earn by holding your tax money and investing it. Always make sure your deductions are substantial enough to support your claims.

Survival Strategies

Planning is the key to reducing the taxes you pay under the Economic Recovery Tax Act. The idea is to take advantage of falling tax rates by:

• First, accelerating tax deductions.

• And, second, deferring income whenever possible and whenever practical.

The idea is that a deduction is worth more when the rate of

21

taxation is higher, and less when the rate is lower. Likewise, a dollar is worth more when it is taxed at a cheaper rate.

Ways of accelerating tax deductions include:

• *Prepaying State and Local Taxes.* Real estate taxes and state income taxes all can be paid in advance—that is, in December, the last month of the year. By doing so, you earn the deduction a year earlier. Consult with the individual who prepares your taxes. He or she can help here in figuring your income tax burden a bit earlier. Also, if you want to know how much your real estate taxes are, simply call the local government office in charge of collecting these. They'll be delighted to help you.

• *Buying Big-Ticket Items Now.* If you plan to purchase a car, a boat or a plane soon, you may want to consider buying it before the end of the tax year. That way, you can deduct the sales tax while the tax rates are higher.

• *Medical and Dental Expenses.* The strategy here is similar to the one involving early purchases of more expensive items. This may sound farfetched, but consider the possibilities. The cost of orthodontia for two teenagers could require a cash outlay of as much as $5,000. Optional plastic surgery to remove the bags under your eyes could carry a price tag of $6,000. A face lift regarded as necessary (the Internal Revenue Service accepts this as an allowable medical expense) may produce a $10,000 deduction.

• *Charitable Contributions.* Charitable organizations won't complain about an early donation. Pay your pledges in advance, or donate that painting worth several thousand dollars to your college library this year and earn your charitable contribution deduction in 1982, when it is worth more. If you are a high earner, consider establishing a charitable lead trust, a vehicle that permits you to deduct now the current value of contributions scheduled to be made during the life of the trust.

The other side of this maneuver—postponing income to 1983 so that it is taxed at a lower rate—may be harder to accomplish. Few of us can afford to defer for any length of time large portions of our salaries. Also, the company employing us may balk at the suggestion that we not be paid until some later date.

Still, if you are a salesman or an executive, you may be able to have your firm delay a December 1982 bonus payment until January 1983, or it may be possible to postpone taking capital gains (more about this in chapter 8). Other possibilities include:

• If you own a family corporation, you may want to re-schedule payment of dividends. Postponing this income until January 1, 1983, may be a sound idea.

• If you plan to invest in fixed-income securities, you may buy obligations for which the payoff comes later: The interest earned on U.S. Treasury bills (a $10,000 minimum investment) and certain delayed certificates of deposit (usually at least $500 to $1,000 are required for these) is not credited until maturity. Be careful here, though, because not all investment vehicles provide for delayed recognition of income earned. Ask the institution or the organization you're purchasing the certificates from. Its officers should be able to answer your questions.

• If for 1981 you are in a tax bracket higher than 50 percent, you may want to postpone short-term earnings on investments—those held less than one year and one day—until after January 1, 1982. At that time, the maximum tax rate on this type of income drops from a ceiling of 70 percent to 50 percent. (More about this in chapter 8.)

A warning: Be careful about deferring income, because you may lose more than you gain. For instance, deferring a $10,000 bonus one year until 1983 will save an executive about $500. By taking the bonus and earning a 15 percent return on it, that same executive makes a gross profit of $1,500, or $1,000 after taxes.

Chapter 3 _____

Breaks for Couples and Singles with Kids

Until the Economic Recovery Tax Act, there was only one way to avoid the "marriage penalty." ("Marriage penalty" is the term used to describe the U.S. Treasury's long-standing practice of taxing at a higher rate the earnings of working married couples than the like income of single persons). Near the end of each December, you and your spouse could fly to some exotic, sand-speckled place, secure a divorce, and then, on the first day of the new year, remarry. By doing so, you could file your federal tax return listing your status as "divorced," and you could pay lower taxes. Then the Treasury ruled that this divorce-and-remarry technique (which some people actually tried) was simply a way of avoiding taxes. If you did it, you could be prosecuted for income tax evasion.

Now there is a partial solution to the problem of the marriage penalty. The government has adopted a new rule for reducing it. The rule is effective beginning in 1982. This new rule is not the only break in the new tax law for married persons or for single people with children. There are new child- and dependent-care provisions, including a little-known fringe benefit that companies can now provide for employees— one well worth knowing and asking about. There are also some new rules relating to charitable contributions that make taking such deductions possible for those taxpayers—usually in more modest tax brackets—who do not itemize their tax deductions. This is an advantage, particularly for many younger married couples.

Eliminating the Marriage Penalty

For those who have been victims of the marriage penalty, a new deduction may be taken beginning with your 1982 income, and that deduction will be expanded for 1983. Thus, the new law is phasing in this relief over two years. The deduction to lessen the marriage penalty is subtracted from gross income, which means that couples who do not itemize their deductions can use the new formula.

Specifically what the new law does for married couples is this:

• 1982. A deduction of 5 percent may be taken from the lower-earning spouse's "qualified earned income" up to $30,000. The maximum deduction for 1982 is $1,500. Note that this refers to the lower-earning spouse's income, not the couple's total earnings. This is a crucial point.

• 1983 and thereafter. A deduction of 10 percent will be allowed, based on the lower-earning spouse's "qualified earned income" up to $30,000. Thus, the maximum annual deduction will be $3,000.

Qualified earned income is defined by the new law as personal service income: salary, wages, tips, bonuses, etc. It does not include income from pensions or annuities, or certain deferred compensation sometimes awarded to corporate executives. Nor does it include wages paid by one spouse to the other, as in a family business. Finally, the qualified earned income must be reduced by deductions taken for the contributions to Individual Retirement Accounts (IRAs) or the Keogh plans of the self-employed.

Here is an illustration of how the marriage penalty relief

provision of the new law works: Harry Atkins earns $25,000 and his wife, Peggy, $20,000, for a combined gross income of $45,000. Their financial picture for 1981, 1982, and 1983 tax years is given in figure 3–1.

FIGURE 3–1

FOR TAX YEAR

	1981	1982	1983
Combined income	$45,000	$45,000	$45,000
Marriage penalty tax relief deduction	0	1,000 (5%)	2,000 (10%)
Itemized deductions	9,850	9,850	9,850
Two personal exemptions (no children)	2,000	2,000	2,000
Taxable income	$33,150	$32,150	$31,150

Under the new marriage penalty provision, the Atkinses, with their taxable income, incur the tax liabilities and breaks shown in figure 3–2.

FIGURE 3–2

	1981	1982	1983
Income tax	$7,311	$6,317	$5,409
Marginal tax bracket	37%	33%	30%
Marriage-penalty tax relief	0	$330	$600

SOURCE: DELOITTE HASKINS & SELLS

It is easy to see from the Atkinses' case that the marriage-penalty relief provision is helpful but not as substantial as it could be. (Compared to the type of tax lures cast out for corporate executives, it is puny bait.) In fact, some of us— even with the new marriage deduction—would save more by getting divorced or by not marrying at all. Consider this example:

James Ball earns $27,500 annually. So does his fiancée, Melinda Lancaster. As singles, each will pay $5,629 in taxes, or a combined total of $11,258, for tax year 1983—the year the marriage penalty relief is fully phased in. If they marry that year and file a joint return, their tax burden will total $12,914—$1,656 above the single rate. Without the change in the law their tax would have been $14,014 as a married couple. Thus, it is obvious that even when the full effect of the marriage penalty relief is in place in 1983, the amount saved falls far short of producing an equitable tax rate.

The uneven results of the marriage penalty relief law no doubt will stir long debate in Washington. At this writing, some members of Congress—many of them among those who supported the new tax law—are quietly working for a recasting of the rules. They also are tackling another related inequity: A married couple, one employed outside the home, the other not but with sizable income from investments, does not qualify for relief from the marriage penalty.

A final point: If you live in a community property state such as California or Texas, you can disregard for federal tax purposes the state-law concept that married people share their personal earnings fifty-fifty. The federal government, from its viewpoint, says this is not so and does not permit use of the fifty-fifty rule in figuring whether you qualify for the marriage penalty relief deduction.

New Breaks on Day Care Costs

There is some good news for working parents: The Economic Recovery Tax Act provides two important new tax breaks that should be of help, and these are effective beginning in 1982. One relates to employers, and the other permits higher personal tax credits to be taken for child- or dependent-care expenses.

First, the new law says that:

• If you are reimbursed by your employer for child-care costs, you need not add this amount to your earnings in computing your taxable income.

• If you are an employer, the money you pay to employees for child-care expenses is deductible as an ordinary and necessary cost of doing business.

• Persons who are only partially compensated by their employers for their child-care costs still may be able personally to claim a tax credit covering the remainder of their expenses.

Here is an illustration of the last point: Barbara Stafford spends $4,000 annually for day care for her two children. Her employer reimburses $2,000, and she pays the remainder of the costs from her salary. She still may be able to claim a personal tax credit covering the $2,000 she pays herself. The word "may" is used here partly because at this writing, the Treasury Department has not yet clarified this section of the law. It should do so by the time you file your 1982 tax return, however, so check with an accountant or the Internal Revenue Service.

These new day-care tax deductions in the Economic Recovery Tax Act are included under the title Dependent Care Assistance Program. It allows companies to take tax deductions if they establish and maintain their own day-care centers for employees on company property, and it also allows deductions to companies that pay the costs of child care either directly to a local day-care center or to the employee whose child is being cared for at such a facility. The only limitations are that for the company to take the deductions, the employee's child receiving the care must be under age 15, and the care must be provided in order that the employee is free to work outside the home.

The inclusion of these tax breaks in the new law should be particularly helpful to working couples with children and to working single parents. Also, the law may benefit individuals with disabled spouses: The new tax law states that if a company reimburses a worker for the care of his disabled spouse, this money need not be added to that person's annual taxable income—the same allowance granted to employees with dependent children.

Child- and Dependent-Care Tax Credit

The second major break for working parents and individuals who are responsible for the care of a loved one (including an elderly parent, or a full-time student, for example) is that the authors of the Economic Recovery Tax Act have extended the scope of what is known as the "child- and dependent-care tax credit." The idea behind this credit is simply that individuals who are working and caring for children or a disabled or incompetent family member incur added expenses and should receive some sort of tax break.

Under the old tax law—and the new law—the credit is a figure subtracted from the amount of tax you owe the federal government at the end of each year. (This makes it more valuable than a tax deduction, which merely reduces the income subject to taxation.) The amount of credit you are permitted to claim does not equal 100 percent of the amount it takes for you to care for your child or your dependent or dependents while you are working. Rather, it follows this schedule:

• 20 percent of the expenses incurred up to $2,000 for caring for one child or one dependent—a maximum credit of $400.

• 20 percent of the expenses incurred up to $4,000 for the care of two or more dependents—a maximum credit of $800.

The law also sets several very simple criteria for determining your eligibility for the credit:

• The expenses incurred must be necessary in order for the taxpayer to be employed away from home.

• You must—if married—file a joint tax return.

• You must maintain a residence for your claimed dependents.

The Treasury considers tuition to private schools to be an improper expense toward this tax credit. Day care provided for youngsters by relatives—a grandmother, for example—qualifies for the tax credit, so long as the relative is not claimed as a dependent (personal exemption) by the child's parent. Thus, it is wise to keep close records of any such payments within the family, in the event of a tax audit.

Other legitimate expenses which can be applied toward the child- and dependent-care credit are these:

• Nursemaid care for children and incapacitated adults.

• Domestic helpers who do cooking, cleaning, laundry, etc., and "keep an eye on the children."

• Babysitters.

• Day-care centers, nursery schools, and day camps in the country—for children under 15 years of age.

The Economic Recovery Tax Act not only retains all these liberal rules but expands upon them:

• Beginning in 1982, expenditures for out-of-home noninstitutional care of a disabled spouse or dependent, who regularly spends at least eight hours a day in the taxpayer's home, are eligible for the credit. Under prior law, services outside the home qualified only if they involved the care of a child under 15 years of age. However, the new law makes it clear that dependent-care centers providing out-of-household services must be in compliance with state and/or local regulations in order for their costs to be deductible.

• If your adjusted gross income is $10,000 or less annually, you may claim a tax credit of 30 percent of expenses involved in caring for your dependent or dependents while you are at your job. The maximum expenses are $2,400 for one dependent and $4,800 for two or more dependents. This means that the top tax credit for individuals earning $10,000 or less each year is $720 for the care of one child or dependent (30 percent times $2,400 equals $720) or $1,440 for the care of two or more dependents (30 percent times $4,800 equals $1,440).

• The 30-percent-of-expenses figure is reduced by one percent for each $2,000 of income (or fraction thereof) for persons earning between $10,000 and $30,000 annually. The ceiling for expenses—$2,400 for one dependent, $4,800 for two or more dependents—remains in effect for persons in these higher income levels, however. This means that if you earned $20,000 each year and claimed you were responsible for paying for the care of one child while you worked, your maximum tax credit would be $600 (.25 times $2,400). The 30 percent figure is reduced to 25 percent because your income of $20,000 is $10,000 above the $10,000 level that justifies a full 30 percent of care expenses. For two or more dependents, your top tax credit would be $1,200, which is 25 percent times $4,800. Likewise, if your annual gross income was $30,000, your tax credit would be 20 percent of $2,400, or $480, for one dependent or 20 percent of $4,800—$960—for the care of two or more persons. Figure 3–3 lists the maximum tax credits available under the new law.

Both the old and the new tax rules providing credits for child and dependent care are liberal. True, you must be employed to take the tax credit, since it is designed to protect your ability to hold a job outside the home. But you can be a part-time employee and qualify for the credit. (It will be less than the maximum, though, since the amount you may deduct is linked to your earnings.) Here is an example:

You are a young widow, employed part-time and earning $50 each week or $2,600 annually. You spend $3,500 a year caring for your children while you are at your job, shopping, doing hospital volunteer work, and such. The credit you are permitted to take equals $780—a figure derived by multiplying 30 percent by $2,600, your annual earnings. (You cannot— although some people try to—compute your tax credit by multiplying the specified percentage times the amount you

FIGURE 3–3

CHILD- AND DEPENDENT-CARE TAX CREDIT: MAXIMUM
DEDUCTIONS

Income	Percentage of Expenses	Maximum Allowable Deduction	
		One Dependent	Two or More Dependents
$10,000	30	$720	$1,440
12,000	29	696	1,392
14,000	28	672	1,344
16,000	27	648	1,296
18,000	26	624	1,248
20,000	25	600	1,200
22,000	24	576	1,152
24,000	23	552	1,104
26,000	22	528	1,056
28,000	21	504	1,008
28,000 plus	20	480	960

spend caring for your dependent. This widow, for example, cannot multiply 30 percent by $3,500.)

The rules regarding child and dependent care also are flexible in their treatment of full-time students and of spouses who are physically or mentally incapable of caring for themselves. The law permits the working marriage partners of incapacitated persons to claim the child- and dependent-care tax credit. Likewise, it allows couples wherein one spouse is employed and the other is a full-time student to take the tax credit. The student is considered employed since he or she is engaged full-time in attending classes and studying. (The Internal Revenue Service defines a full-time student as one attending school or college at least five months a year and enrolled in at least 12 hours of classwork each week.) There is one catch: If both a husband and a wife are full-time students and neither of them is employed, they are *not* allowed to claim a child- or dependent-care tax credit. If you are in this situation, you may want to consider a part-time job, because it would permit you to qualify for this tax credit.

For divorced parents, a special rule is provided regarding the credit. That rule states that the parent having legal custody of the child or children may alone claim the child-care tax credit. The noncustodial parent claims nothing, even if he or she bears some child-care expenses. Parents with joint custody split the child-care credit fifty-fifty.

One limitation attached to the child-dependent-care credit is that it is what the law calls a "nonrefundable" credit. That is, you cannot carry over the credit from one tax year to the next, as in the case of some other types of tax credits. This credit amounts to a simple one-year transaction and cannot be used in later years to offset more substantial income.

Still confused by the child- and dependent-care credit? Consider these two examples:

• John and Joan Hill are a working couple with two small children. He earns $22,500 annually, and her income totals $12,500 each year, for a combined income of $35,000. The children's grandparents do not wish to serve as full-time baby-sitters, so the Hills hire a college student to serve as "nannie" and pay her $15 a day for a five-day week. She works 50 weeks during 1982, bringing the total cost of child care for the Hills to $3,750.

The Hills, of course, qualify for a child-care tax credit. That credit is figured on the basis of Mrs. Hill's $12,500-a-year salary. (The law states that when both a husband and wife work, only one of their salaries is used in computing the credit, and the law permits the lesser salary to be used.) Thus, the Hills's tax credit equals 28 percent times $3,750—or $1,050, with 28 percent used because Joan Hill's income—at $12,500—is $2,500 above the $10,000 income level that would allow the full 30 percent credit. Had the Hills but one child and

COUPLES AND SINGLES WITH KIDS

their child-care costs remained the same, their credit would have equaled 28 percent (once again) times $2,400, which is the maximum expense under the formula for one youngster. The credit: $672.

• Elaine Past is a widow with two youngsters. Elaine's mother lives with her and is confined to her bed. Elaine is employed as the chief buyer for a large metropolitan department store and earns a salary of $40,000 in 1982. She also receives an $18,000 bonus, bringing her total income to $58,000. To be employed, Elaine must make provisions for the care of her mother and her two children: She pays a woman who lives nearby $25 each week to serve a simple lunch to her mother and to look in on her periodically. She spends $40 a week for each of her children—$80 total—to be cared for at a local day-care center after the two are dismissed from kindergarten classes at noon.

Elaine's child- and dependent-care tax credit is computed this way: Her total expense is $25 times 50 weeks, or a cost of $1,250 in 1982 for caring for her mother. For her children, she spends $80 times 50 weeks, or a total of $4,000. (Both types of expenses are allowable under the tax credit rules. It makes no difference that the expense incurred for the children was paid to an agency not operating in the home.) Elaine's total expenses for caring for her dependents is $1,250 (her mother) plus $4,000 (the two children), and that equals $5,250. Her tax credit is 20 percent (the level for persons earning in excess of $28,000) times $4,800 (the maximum allowable expenses for two or more persons), or a total of $960.

Tax Breaks for Persons Adopting Children

Adopting a child becomes less onerous under a new tax break, effective retroactively to January 1, 1981. What that tax break does is this:

• It allows you to deduct up to $1,500 of the expenses

incurred in the course of adopting a child if that child is one "with special needs," meaning one who is receiving some sort of maintenance assistance funds under federal law. If you have questions about whether you qualify, check with your adoption agency. This deduction is an itemized one and consequently is not available to persons filing a short-form 1040.

• It allows you to include as part of your deduction reasonable adoption fees charged by an adoption agency and attorney fees and court costs if these are clearly related to the adoption.

New Rules Regarding Charitable Contributions

Although Americans are noted for their generous charitable contributions, the amount we have donated—on a per-person basis—has declined during the past decade. No one is quite sure why—perhaps it has been inflation; perhaps high taxes; perhaps because contributions could never be deducted by the millions of people who do not itemize their tax deductions. Regardless, the Economic Recovery Tax Act has made changes, and these should help individuals who give regularly to religious groups, hospitals, and other charities. Young married couples who have children and who, because they are generous—or sometimes owing to community pressures—donate to charity throughout the year, stand to benefit most from the changes in the tax law.

The new law allows you to deduct for donations even if you do not itemize your medical, state and local tax, interest expense, and other tax deductions. Now you can file a short-form 1040 and still obtain a deduction for charitable donations. Of course, if you do itemize, the problem does not exist: You can, as always, claim the deductions, assuming you have evidence of the gifts in case the IRS questions you.

Positive as this sounds, there is a problem with this part of the new tax law. While it eliminates your need to itemize to obtain donation deductions, it does not permit you to deduct the entire amount until 1986. On the contrary, the law sets a strict schedule telling how much you may deduct on a percentage basis from 1982 through 1986, as follows:

• 1982. Single persons and married couples filing joint tax returns may deduct 25 percent of the first $100 of charitable contributions, even if they do not itemize. Married persons filing separate returns may each deduct 12.5 percent of the first $100, even if they do not itemize.

• 1983. Deductions follow the same rules.

• 1984. The tax law increases the allowable deductions for married couples filing joint returns and single persons to 25 percent of the first $300 contributed. Married individuals filing separate returns each may subtract 12.5 percent of their first $300 of charitable giving.

• 1985. Married couples filing individual or joint returns and single persons may claim on their federal income tax returns 50 percent of all their charitable contributions.

• 1986. The law permits each of us—regardless of our marital status and how we file our income taxes—to deduct 100 percent of all the charitable contributions we make.

As has been noted, the new tax break on contributions ends at the close of 1986. It could, of course, be renewed by Congress.

Chapter 4

Blessings for All-Savers

The "All-Savers" Certificate is sold by savings banks, commercial banks, savings and loan companies and some company credit unions. The benefits are not as large as you might imagine—if you're judging by all the hoopla—yet the certificates are worth knowing about. Even a dollar of clear profit these days is worth something. And the certificates *are* another option in the span of possibilities in the presently active money market.

Beware, though, for there is fine print in the law (you can get tripped up, for instance, if you use borrowed funds to buy the certificates), and some gimmickry has been practiced by some savings and loan companies that should know better. You ought to be aware of this, as well.

Why All-Savers Certificates Were Created

Savings and loan and similar institutions are in trouble. They have been since 1978, when interest rates began their traumatic rise and depositors—seduced by high money market rates—began withdrawing their savings from passbook accounts and moving those funds into other investment vehicles.

The crisis the crunch savings institutions find themselves in can be illustrated with the case of a single individual:

Sam McBrayer has an 8-year-old 25-year mortgage on his brick house. The interest rate on that mortgage is pegged at a low 9 percent, tying down the bank for the next 17 years and placing it in a near-impossible bind. How can the bank—on the one hand—pay 15 percent for most of its funds and at the same time accept McBrayer's monthly mortgage check based on 9 percent?

Moreover, if you view McBrayer as a depositor in the savings and loan or bank, why should he let his hard-to-come-by savings ride in the lender's vault at the old low interest rate—some 5 percent or so—set years ago for savings accounts when he can earn 10 percent to 20 percent elsewhere? (McBrayer's bank sells $10,000 certificates at high rates of interest, of course, and this helps balance the situation, but only marginally.) The answer is that McBrayer should *not* permit his money to remain in such below-market bank and savings and loan accounts. He should put his funds into instruments providing a higher interest rate, such as money market mutual funds paying 15 percent or more. And he does just that.

What makes McBrayer's case important is that it is typical: Millions of Americans hold reasonably low-interest home mortgage loans from savings institutions. At the same time, millions of Americans have removed their money from these organizations, using their funds to purchase higher-yielding investment certificates. The institutions' assets are thereby being depleted.

All this has prompted bankers to seek the government's help. In response, the Reagan Administration has created all-savers certificates—investment devices designed to halt the flow of deposits out of certain financial institutions, to encourage saving and to provide money for home mortgages.

Defining All-Savers Certificates

The Economic Recovery Tax Act allows financial institutions to issue tax-exempt savings certificates. One requirement is that specified amounts of the proceeds from these certificates must be invested by the institutions issuing them in residential mortgages or agricultural loans.

The interest rates paid on the certificates is set indirectly by the federal government. The U.S. Department of the Treasury fixes rates on the investment certificates it sells—known as Treasury bills—on a weekly basis. The Reagan tax law states that the interest on all-savers certificates will equal 70 percent of the percentage paid on T-bills. Thus, the interest you receive may vary depending on the time you buy all-savers certificates.

Also according to the law, the certificates must carry a one-year maturity. They began to be issued—in denominations of $500—on October 1, 1981, and sales are scheduled to end on December 31, 1982. Because of their one-year length, the last certificates will mature by December 31, 1983.

The benefits for the nation's taxpayers are these: Single individuals will not be taxed on a total of $1,000 of interest income over the period in which these qualifying certificates are outstanding. Married persons filing a joint return may exempt up to $2,000 of interest income. To this limited extent, the certificates are tax-free.

It is important that you invest no more in the certificates than will earn you your $1,000 (if you are single) or your $2,000 (if you are married), since the certificates pay interest below top money market rates. To determine how much you should invest, first find out what rate of interest the certificates are paying, then multiply that percentage by $500—the denomination of the certificates (15 percent times $500, for example). Divide the answer (15 percent times $500 equals $75) into the amount of interest you are permitted to earn tax-free ($1,000 divided by $75). The result is the number of $500 all-savers certificates you will need to buy to earn the tax-free amount ($1,000 divided by $75 equals 13.3).

Regarding all-savers certificates, the important point to remember here is the time factor. The $1,000 or $2,000 in tax-free income applies *not* to each tax year but for the length of the program; i.e., October 1, 1981, to December 31, 1983. If a taxpayer earns interest over and above the excludable amount only the first interest earned is exempt from taxation. Three illustrations:

• Lou Harrison owns some of the $500 certificates, and in 1982 he earns $750 in interest, and, in 1983, he receives $550 in interest income. He may exclude from taxation $750 of this income for 1982, and $250 of the $550 in 1983—for a $1,000 total, the maximum allowed for a single taxpayer.

• Karen Ryan purchases several of the $500 certificates. Her interest earnings total $950 in 1982 and $720 in 1983. She exempts from taxation the $950 on her 1982 tax return. That leaves only $50 of her interest income excluded from taxation in 1983.

• Bill Fields buys a number of $500 all-savers certificates from his local savings and loan association. In 1982 his interest earnings total $800; in 1983, that figure climbs to $1,400. On his 1982 tax return, the $800 is excluded from earnings. On his 1983 return, $1,200 of interest income is exempt. The reason for these larger deductions is that Fields—unlike Harrison and Ryan—is married.

Another important point to remember about all-savers certificates is that the $2,000 limitation—available in the case of married persons filing joint returns—is applicable even when all the interest is earned by one of the individuals. Each person is treated as earning one-half of the total amount. This may be significant where taxpayers file a joint return in one year and separate returns or joint returns with other individuals in another year. (Yes, this is a built-in tax advantage for married persons, but it simply duplicates similar provisions in other parts of the federal tax code.)

Consider this example:

Brent Hamilton decides that the all-savers certificates are for him and purchases enough of them to pay interest totaling $700 in 1982. He excludes the $700 from his taxable income when he files his return in the spring of 1983.

Meanwhile, Hamilton's fiancée—Brenda Smith—has similar ideas and tucks away enough cash from her paychecks to buy similar certificates. She, too, excludes $700 from taxable income for 1982.

The following June, in 1983, Hamilton and Smith are married, and in 1983 both are paid $700 in interest on their individually held certificates—a total of $1,400.

The two possible results:

• Hamilton and Smith file a joint tax return for 1983, as a working couple, and exclude from their taxable income $600—the proper amount, since they must subtract the $1,400 previously excluded by them in 1982 from the $2,000 maximum allowed a married couple.

• Hamilton and Smith file separate tax returns for 1983, and each of them excludes $300 for the year—$1,000 minus $700, the proper amount in line with the $1,000 maximum for single persons.

Strings Are Attached

One major drawback of the all-savers certificates is that if any portion of a certificate is redeemed or disposed of before maturity, the exclusion from taxable income is not available for any interest earned on that certificate. Interest which has been properly excluded in an earlier year must be included as income in the year the certificate is prematurely disposed of or redeemed. Using any portion of a certificate as collateral or security for a loan will be treated by the IRS as a redemption of the whole certificate.

Clearly, the new law takes a hard shot at investors who sell their investments—no matter the reason—before the year is out. This is parallel to the strict penalties enforced by savings and loan institutions against depositors who prematurely withdraw funds placed in their time accounts. Before buying these certificates, make certain that you can afford to put aside the cash for the set one-year period. Remember that you can get good money-market interest rates on your savings by purchasing other types of investments not requiring such a "long hold." There is no comparable penalty for an investor in Treasury bills or short-term notes, and it becomes an issue to weigh when deciding what to buy. Early redemption can wipe away the certificates' entire advantage.

Another catch in purchasing all-savers certificates is how you finance them: Borrowing to buy a tax-exempt investment is a no-no where the Internal Revenue Service is concerned. For years this has raised a fuss and created many tax court cases—most of them resolved in favor of the government. The idea is that if you—as an individual taxpayer—get one big break from Uncle Sam—namely, a free ride on taxation of investments such as municipal bonds issued by a state or local government—you should *not* receive a second break simultaneously. You should not have the right to take a deduction for the interest paid on a loan drawn to cover the purchase of tax-free securities. The government says you can't have it both ways: you cannot get tax-free income *and* the advantage of an interest deduction arising from the same deal. You earn the tax-free income, but you forgo the interest deduction.

Another limitation to all-savers certificates is that interest paid on these investments is excludable from taxable income only by individual taxpayers or by estates of descendants receiving the certificates. Interest paid on the certificates is treated as taxable income if it is paid to trusts, to corporations or to Sub-Chapter S corporations (usually a family-owned corporation, taxed as if it were a proprietorship).

What this means is that if you set up a trust for a member of your family (a trust, for instance, listing a bank as the trustee and a child as the beneficiary), the interest from your all-savers certificates is not subject to tax exemption. It also means that if you own a Sub-Chapter S corporation, you lose. With this type of company, the owners or stockholders make an "election" with the IRS that they personally, instead of the corporation, will report and pay taxes on any corporate profits. It is a way for individuals to obtain the nontax advantages of a corporation—such as limited personal liability in a lawsuit—without having to pay taxes under the corporate rate structure.

Neither the exclusion for trusts nor sub-Chapter S corporations are major problems for most of us—but they are part of the picture.

Should You Invest in an All-Savers Certificate?

The net proceeds all-savers certificates produce for taxpayers is modest—when you compare a $10,000 investment in these certificates with $10,000 put into a Treasury bill—as we explain below. But Treasury bills are sold only in $10,000 denominations—none smaller, none larger, although you can purchase as many as you wish. The price, however, places them out of the reach of many individuals.

The result is that many small investors, including young married couples with just a few thousand saved, may find the all-savers certificates attractive: They provide some meaningful way of saving vis-à-vis conventional bank accounts and savings and loan accounts. However, they may not be quite as alluring when compared with other investment possibilities, as will be explained later.

Should you invest in an all-savers certificate with its lim-

Figure 4–1

PROJECTED YIELDS: 12.6 PERCENT ALL-SAVERS
CERTIFICATES

Single Taxpayer's Taxable Income	Tax Bracket	Equals a Taxable Return of:
$12,900 to $15,000	26%	17.04%
15,000 to 18,200	30	17.51
18,200 to 23,500	34	19.11
23,500 to 28,800	39	20.67
28,800 to 34,100	44	22.52
34,100 to 41,500	49	24.73
41,500 to 55,300	55	28.02
55,300 to 81,800	63	34.08

SOURCE: U.S. LEAGUE OF SAVINGS ASSOCIATIONS

ited tax-free income attached or in a taxable Treasury bill or in a taxable bank savings certificate or in a money market mutual fund?

Take a look at figures 4–1 and 4–2.

Whether you should invest in all-savers certificates depends primarily on your income tax bracket—as figures 4–1 and 4–2 illustrate. Speaking generally, only taxpayers in marginal brackets above 30 percent will pick up a greater after-tax return on the all-savers certificates than on Treasury bills or most money market investments: The 30 percent level is when the $1,000 tax-free exclusion of the certificates is equal to the

FIGURE 4–2

PROJECTED YIELDS: 12.6 PERCENT ALL-SAVERS
CERTIFICATE

Married Taxpayer's Taxable Income	Tax Bracket	Equals a Taxable Return of:
$20,200 to $24,600	28%	17.51%
24,600 to 29,900	32	18.54
29,900 to 35,200	37	20.02
35,200 to 45,800	43	22.12
45,800 to 60,000	49	24.73
60,000 to 85,600	54	27.41
85,600 to 109,400	59	30.76
109,400 to 162,400	64	35.03

SOURCE: U.S. LEAGUE OF SAVINGS ASSOCIATIONS

return on other investment vehicles. Below that level, you can earn more on other investments: All-savers certificates are pegged to pay just 70 percent of the fifty-two-week Treasury bill yield.

Here is an example:

First, let's assume that you are reasonably well off and are not hampered by having only a few thousand dollars or less to invest. In fact, let's assume that you have $10,000 in your checking account and you are trying to decide just what to do with it. Let's also pretend that you are single and in a 40 percent tax bracket in 1982. That means your taxable income ranges between $28,800 and $34,100. (If you were married and in this bracket, your joint return would list earnings between $35,200 and $45,800.) During the current year, you earn exactly $30,000.

In trying to decide whether to put your $10,000 into a fifty-two-week Treasury bill yielding a modest 14.3 percent or into an all-savers certificate earning 10.01 percent (that is the result of 70 percent times 14.3 percent), you produce these figures:

A Treasury Bill. If you invest in this vehicle, you will earn interest income of $1,430. Under your 40 percent tax rate, you pay $572 on your earnings, meaning you have an after-tax profit of $858.

All-Savers Certificates. You invest in this device and receive interest totaling $1,001. No tax is levied on that amount, so you pocket it all.

In this illustration, you earn an extra $143 by investing in all-savers certificates rather than purchasing the higher-yielding Treasury bill. But here's another example:

This time pretend you're still single but you earn less money. You've dropped into a 30 percent tax bracket. As a result, a $10,000 investment in a Treasury bill yields $1,430 in interest at maturity. Your tax liability on that amount is $429, bringing your after-tax profit to $1,001—equal to the net return on the all-savers certificate.

The lessons of these two illustrations are these:

• It is smart to buy all-savers certificates if you are in a bracket above 30 percent—over $18,000 in taxable income in 1982 if you are single or over $25,000 if filing a joint return.

• It makes little sense to buy an all-savers certificate if you have at least $10,000 to invest and are in the 30 percent or less marginal tax bracket. Place your money elsewhere. All-savers certificates for you are a wash, a standoff, compared with putting your money into a $10,000 Treasury bill. Further, by not investing in the all-savers devices, you won't have the added disadvantages involving stiff penalties for early sale or redemption.

There is a third lesson, too: Don't forget to shop for your investments. Before opting to purchase any vehicle, compare the current fifty-two-week Treasury bill yield and the 70 percent all-savers after-tax income. Then examine:

• The earnings from six-month bank savings certificates, available in $10,000 units, and

• The profits available through money market mutual fund shares, sold by such firms as Dreyfus, Merrill Lynch, Oppenheimer, Rowe Price. These are the companies that have hurt the banks and savings and loans by drawing off their deposits.

Keep in mind that the six-month bank savings certificates, which pay fully taxable income, are pegged to the current Treasury bill rate, while the money market mutual funds—which invest wholly in liquid paper such as big-volume bank certificates and high-paying corporate notes—usually pay a yield that is fractionally higher.

For instance, in one recent week, there were these differences in the rates being paid:

• Treasury bills (52-week) yielded 18 percent.

• All-savers certificates, for those in the 25 percent tax bracket, yielded 16.8 percent.

• All-savers certificates for individuals in the 40 percent tax bracket paid 21 percent.

• All-savers certificates, for persons in the 50 percent tax bracket, produced 25 percent interest.

• Six-month bank certificates yielded 16.9 percent.

• Money market mutual funds (the average) earned 17.1 percent.

Investment options available obviously are varied—even if you have less than $10,000 to invest. Explore them all.

IRS Ruling

If you bought all-savers certificates last year, keep in mind an IRS edict issued September 4, 1981. The ruling was made in 1981—after the availability of the new all-savers certificates was announced but before their actual issuance on October 1. It was issued because many banks and savings and loan institutions began selling what are referred to as "repurchase agreements."

These contracts provided high short-term interest rates to people who agreed to reinvest their money in the new tax-free all-savers certificates on October 1. The offering of inflated short-term interest was a kind of bribe—to get savers to put their money into particular banks or savings and loans versus other institutions. The scheme backfired.

The Internal Revenue Service announced that it had grave doubts about the taxability of the certificates sold on this basis and implied that the buyers might lose the tax-free feature. People panicked and began calling their banks and congressmen. Then came IRS Ruling 81-218. The nation's tax collectors said, in effect, that in many cases the all-savers certificates tied to a repurchase agreement would lose their tax-free status. The instances in which the tax breaks are lost involve repurchase agreements promising side benefits such as more favorable terms for consumer or mortgage loans.

If this sounds muddled, indeed it is. The best idea if you bought one of these certificates prior to their actual issuance is to check with a tax advisor. This is especially important if you received any special come-on benefits such as those mentioned here.

A brighter note: The IRS also has ruled that the "rollover" of a six-month bank savings certificate into an all-savers certificate is a legitimate move. The $1,000–$2,000 exclusion of all-savers income would not be tainted through this method.

Dividend and Interest Exclusion

Another item of interest in the new Reagan tax law is the short-term change regarding the exclusion of dividend and interest from your taxable income. Prior to 1981, taxpayers were permitted to exempt up to $100 ($200 on a joint return) of dividend income annually. For 1981 and 1982, this exclusion has been expanded to include interest income. Additionally, the amount of exclusion has increased for one year to $200 on a single return and $400 on a joint return.

The specific changes the new law makes are these:

1981. During that tax year, the law permits single persons to exempt $200 and married persons filing a joint return $400 of dividend and interest income. You pay no taxes on these amounts! This is a point to keep in mind if you have not already filed your 1981 tax return.

1982 and thereafter. The tax law allows single people to deduct $100 and married individuals filing a joint return to subtract $200 of dividends. A small amount, granted, but all tax-free income is welcomed.

1985. Beginning in 1985, a new interest exclusion of 15 percent of the excess of interest income over "qualified interest expense" is provided. The maximum deductible is $450 for a single person, $900 for a married couple filing a joint return.

Qualified interest expense does not include: interest on debts incurred to acquire, construct, reconstruct or rehabilitate a dwelling of the taxpayer; interest incurred in the taxpayer's trade or business; or interest on indebtedness incurred to make deposits or investments, to the extent that the interest on such deposits or investments is excludible from gross income. It does include all other types of interest.

An example:

You are a married taxpayer filing a joint return. In 1985 you list the total of $5,900 in interest income:

- $200 received from a savings account in a bank.
- $4,500 received on deposits in a savings and loan.
- $1,200 received from taxable bonds.

At the same time, you list a number of interest expenses (the total is $5,950):

- $4,000 paid to a savings and loan as interest on your home mortgage.
- $1,600 paid to a finance company for the purchase of a boat.
- $350 paid for department store credit accounts and other consumer loans.

You subtract the $4,000 from the $5,950, and you get $1,950, the "qualified interest expense." (As previously noted, the cost of a home mortgage interest is excluded under IRS rules.) You then use the formula provided by the federal government: 15 percent of the total interest income minus interest expense. In this case, 15 percent times $1,950. Your answer is $292.50.

The next step is to multiply that figure by your tax bracket. That gives you the amount you may exclude from taxable income. You are in a 38 percent marginal bracket, so your exclusion equals $111.15 (38 percent times $292.50).

What this example shows is that for most taxpayers, the 15 percent exclusion is a pleasant surprise but merely a tiny bonanza. Changes in the tax law of this sort are trumpeted by the government as a boon to millions, as something for the small investor, something "big" for the "little guy." Actually, such measures bring little relief.

Break for Utility Stockholders

Under the new tax law, shareholders in public utility companies may elect to exclude $750 (single return) or $1,500 (joint return) of certain common stock shares they receive under a plan permitting them to take either stock dividends or cash. The rule applies from 1982 through 1985. If you own an interest in a utility, check this murky provision with the financial office of the utility company before filing your form 1040.

Beware

A final warning about the all-savers certificates: Remember that they must be held for a full year for the tax break to apply. Moreover, check on the insurability of these certificates. At this writing, it isn't certain whether they will have the advantage of federal deposit guarantees.

Chapter 5 _____

The Real Estate Bonanza

Because homes are investments, they are subject to a variety of tax consequences. Overall, the tax laws treat home ownership favorably. The reason for that is the long-standing philosophy of the federal government that says people with houses deserve some sort of tax protection.

The Economic Recovery Tax Act of 1981 does not alter this policy. Indeed, the new law expands upon the notion by providing a number of new tax breaks for homeowners. Among these are the relaxation of regulations governing the sale of a principal residence by a person 55 years of age or older, and the loosening of rules pertaining to the sale of a principal residence by an individual of any age.

"Principal residence" is defined liberally under the new tax law. It may be a house, a condominium, or a cooperative apartment. Probably a mobile home qualifies, too, although the IRS has not specifically said so. If you own a mobile home and wish to make use of this part of the new tax law, check with an accountant or your local IRS office before trying to do so.

Still, principal residences are not the only types of property benefiting under the Economic Recovery Tax Act. New advantageous rules—extensive ones—covering investments in such varied types of real estate as rental condominiums and shopping centers are provided, too. These benefits are among the most liberal of the new tax law.

Let's examine all of them—one at a time.

A Break for Homeowners Age 55 or Older

Mary Stratton is a 64-year-old widow who owes no money on her house, having paid the balance of the mortgage at the time of her husband's death. Weary of property taxes and the expense of maintaining her aging home, she decides to sell the house and move into an apartment building near her daughter's house. She contacts a real estate agent and learns that her property—inherited 40 years before—is worth $110,000. She places it on the market and sells it at that price.

What are the tax consequences for Mrs. Stratton?

The answer—simply stated—is none. Mrs. Stratton, under the new tax law, owes no taxes as a result of selling her home—even if her profit is the full $110,000. It does not matter to the Internal Revenue Service whether she uses the proceeds from the sale to buy another house, places the entire amount in a savings account, or stuffs the money into a glass jar. She owes no taxes.

Why? The Economic Recovery Tax Act says that certain taxpayers may sell their principal residence anytime after July 20, 1981, and pocket the profit tax-free—if certain criteria are met:

• The individual selling his or her principal residence must be 55 years of age or older. The tax law treats a married couple filing a joint return as one person. This means that a couple qualifies for the tax break if only one spouse—the husband or the wife—is 55 or older at the time of the sale. The law also requires that both marriage partners agree in writing to take advantage of this portion of the law. (The requisite form is provided by the IRS, as explained below.)

• The tax-free profit on the sale of the residence—for a

single person or for a married couple filing a joint return—may not exceed $125,000. The top is $62,500 per spouse in the case of a married couple filing separate returns. This follows the law's treatment of a married couple as a single entity. Any capital gain on the house above $125,000 is taxed at the capital gains rate (40 percent of gain subject to ordinary income tax).

• The house sold must have served as the individual's principal residence for at least three years of the preceding five years, with that five-year period ending on the day of the sale. There is one exception to this: If you sold your home prior to July 20, 1981, and you were 65 years of age or older, you may make use of another rule. In this case, you qualify for the tax break if you owned and used your home for five of the past eight years prior to the sale, with that eight-year period ending on the date of the sale.

• The person excluding such a profit from taxable income must *not* have previously taken advantage of this section of the tax law. The maximum $125,000 exclusion from tax is a one-time, once-in-a-lifetime offer.

• You must inform the Internal Revenue Service—via the tax form it provides—of the sale of your principal residence and of your decision to make use of this part of the law. The IRS calls this "making a formal declaration," and it is the government's way of making sure you don't capture the tax break more than once. The required "formal declaration" actually is a government-printed, government-provided form, telling the IRS you have sold your home and how much profit you made by doing so. The form is simple, and there is no need for you to hire a tax preparer to fill it out for you, although you may find it more convenient to do so. If you wish to complete the form yourself, just stop by or telephone your local Internal Revenue Service office and ask for tax form 2119. They will provide you with the form with instructions on how to prepare it, and offer individual assistance if you need it.

How the new law varies from past tax law in its treatment

of the sale of residences by persons 55 years of age or older is simple: Previously, homeowners who sold their principal residence were limited to a tax-free profit of $100,000 ($50,000 in the case of a married person filing a separate return).

But at either the $100,000 or the $125,000 level, this section of the law is a plus. In fact, it is wise, if you are nearing age 55 and considering selling your home, not to put your property on the market until you reach that key age. An alternative is to enter into a sales contract with the buyer specifying that you will sell the property for a specified price, but setting the actual sales date after your 55th birthday.

The point to keep in mind in such a case is the timing to make use of this part of the law. Plan carefully for it because the tax exclusion is far too valuable to waste. Consider this example:

In early 1962, John and Barbara Edwards bought a house for $30,000. By 1982 both of the Edwardses were over 55 years of age. They decide to sell their house, invest the tax-free profit in securities, and move to the Florida vacation cottage they purchased some years earlier.

The price paid for their house is $80,000. From that, the Edwardses subtract the original cost plus selling expenses and a 6 percent real estate agent's commission. Their net profit on the sale is $43,000. They notify the Internal Revenue Service that they intend to make use of the one-time, age-55, home-sale exclusion, and they invest their $43,000 and move South.

All this sounds quite attractive, until you consider one point: The Edwardses used only $43,000 of the allowed exclusion of $125,000 of gain on the sale. The difference between the amount they used and the amount allowed—$82,000—cannot be recouped. The law permits taxpayers to make use of the exclusion only once. This is fine if you can exclude the maximum amount allowable or close to it. But even if you can't, you cannot exclude the difference later on. For the Edwardses it might have been wise to consider, at least, waiting a year or two before selling their home. By then, the housing market might have become stronger, producing a better price while enabling them to take fuller advantage of the $125,000 exclusion.

Happily, the Edwardses can change their minds. The law allows them or anyone else the right to make a new decision. It says that you can cancel your previously filed intention to make use of the age-55-and-older home-sale tax break. However, you must notify the Internal Revenue Service of such a decision within three years following April 15 of the year in which you sell your principal residence.

Why an individual would make use of this option, then change his or her mind is not hard to understand. The most common reason is that a person decides to purchase another "principal residence." By doing so, he or she may be able to avoid taxes on the transaction and at the same time not use the one-time exclusion. This second tax break is available to any homeowner who sells his principal residence and reinvests the money in another home costing as much or more. It is a plum found, indeed—with the advantage extended by the new law—and is provided regardless of the age of the home seller.

Liberalizing Home-Sale Rules

For years, federal law has enabled any homeowner to avoid paying taxes on the proceeds from the sale of a principal residence *if* the money is used to buy another home. The key is the cost of the new house and the timing of the transaction. Both the old law and the new say that homeowners must purchase another residence for an amount at least as great as the selling price of the previous home. The old law also provided that the new residence must be bought within a period beginning 18 months before the sale of the old house and ending 18 months after the sale. Thus, the grace period—up until July 20, 1981—ran three years.

Easier restrictions are provided under the new tax package. First, to make use of this break you still must purchase another residence for a cost equal to or greater than the selling price of your old home. However, the timetable for buying another principal residence is made more liberal. The Economic Recovery Tax Act extends the reinvestment time period to two years before and two years after the sale of your old residence, and thus the grace period is increased to four years.

Transactions subject to the new tax law are those with sale dates after July 20, 1981. You may also qualify if you sold your house prior to that date if the previously allowable 18-month grace period had not expired. An example: You sold your principal residence on May 1, 1981. By July 20, 1981, less than three months passed. Therefore, you would qualify for coverage under the new law because the allowed 18 months had not ended. Your reinvestment time-period automatically is extended to a total of 24 months following the date of sale.

An important point to remember here is that this section of the law—like the one governing the sale of a home by a person age 55 or older—applies only to an individual's principal residence. A vacation cottage occupied by you one month a year, would not qualify. However, a condominium, an apartment, or even a houseboat qualifies—*if* you actually live there. The key is not the type of dwelling you sell or buy but whether you make it your primary place of residence.

Also keep in mind that the location of the home you are selling or the home you are buying is not important. Mainly, you will have your principal residence in the United States, of course; but you qualify for favorable tax treatment under the law even if you live abroad. For instance, your new house may be located in Cuernavaca or Malaga and still you can take advantage of the tax-free transaction.

Thus far, taking advantage of this real estate section of the new tax law sounds simple. It can be—but often there are complicating factors. Consider this example:

You are a young executive transferred to another division of your corporation located in another city. You put your home up for sale and, at the same time, sign a contract to purchase a house for a slightly higher price in a suburb of the new city. You assume that you will be able to sell your old house at about the same time you are scheduled to move into the new house. It doesn't work out that way. The housing market in your old neighborhood is depressed, and although you have several possible buyers interested in the property, you have no firm offers from any of them. You rent the house out until, some six months later, you find a buyer.

Doing this might cause you problems with the Internal Revenue Service because to defer the gain on the sale of a home, it must be your principal residence at the time of the sale. The question that arises, under the circumstances described here, is whether the home—your old home which is being rented—may be considered to be your principal residence when it has been occupied by a tenant. You are not living in it, and occupancy is the test for residence. In response to such cases, the IRS has ruled that a home rented during the period the owner tried to sell it qualifies for deferral of the gain—a tax-free rollover, as it is sometimes called—when the owner meets four criteria:

• He or she intended at all times to sell the house.
• He or she actively pursued a plan to sell the house (engaged a real estate broker, advertised it, and such).
• He or she rented the house only after efforts to effect an immediate sale failed, and
• He or she encouraged the tenant to buy the house by including an option to purchase in the lease—this, a hard rule, indeed.

A good way to avoid trouble with these requirements and safeguard your tax-free sale-and-purchase is this: Buy your new home and then rent it to a tenant temporarily. Take the time needed to sell your old house and then move to your new residence. In this way, there is no question that your old house was your principal residence on the date of the sale.

Another problem in making use of this portion of the tax law occurs when the new residence you purchase costs less than the selling price of the old one. Here is an example:

Bob Williams, a commuter to New York City, is age 52 and his wife, Doris, is 50. Their children have moved away, and Bob, weary of his daily 90-minute commute into Manhattan, suggests that they sell their ten-room house in New Jersey and purchase a condominium near his midtown office in the city. His wife agrees, and they put their New Jersey home on the market.

A buyer offers $110,000, and they are pleased since they had purchased the house for $60,000 only 10 years before. They sign a contract and pay the real estate agent a 6 percent commission—a total of $6,600. That leaves them with a net selling price of $103,400—an amount they believe is sufficient to purchase a small condominium in a pleasant New York City neighborhood. They begin looking but find nothing they like.

They decide to move temporarily into a rental apartment in Manhattan. A year later, they locate a suitable property. Its price: $80,000 or $23,400 less than the net selling price of their home in New Jersey. The tabulation below shows what their balance sheet on the transaction looks like:

- The original purchase price
  of the New Jersey house: $ 60,000

- The gross selling price of
  the New Jersey home: 110,000
  The real estate agent's
  commission plus selling expenses: 6,600

- The net selling price of
  the New Jersey house: 103,400

- The profit on the sale
  of the New Jersey house
  (net selling price minus
  the original purchase
  price):   43,400

- The cost of the
  condominium in Manhattan: 80,000

- Taxable gain on the transaction
  (the net selling price minus
  the cost of the new condominium): $ 23,400

What these figures mean to Bob and Doris Williams is this: Because they paid less for their new principal residence than the selling price of the previous one, they must report a profit on their federal income tax return—in their case, $23,400. Had they paid an amount equal to or greater than the selling price of their previous home, their profit—in the view of the Internal Revenue Service—would have been zero, and they would have owed no tax.

The only good tax news for Bob and Doris is that their profit qualifies as a long-term capital gain, taxable at the low capital gains rate, which is imposed on profits from investments held for more than one year. Computing capital gains tax is explained in chapter 8.

Note: As suggested earlier, a possible alternative for couples in the Williamses' age bracket (early fifties) is to wait until one spouse reaches age 55 to make a home sale. In that way, no capital gains problems need arise.

Another potential complication in making use of this section of the Economic Recovery Tax Act involves taxpayers who are building new homes. If you hire an architect or a contractor to build a house, or contract the work yourself, you still must move into the new residence during the established time frame—within two years before or two years after the sale of your old home. The IRS is strict on this point—despite house-building delays people suffer—and has been supported in a number of cases by the U.S. Tax Court. One reason for the new law's easing of the timing rules for residential realty sales is that many homeowners—like the Williams couple—have been caught in poorly timed transactions.

Breaks for Real Estate Investors

While homeowners enjoy limited gains under the Economic Recovery Tax Act, pure investors in real estate—those who choose to buy commercial, industrial, and rental properties with their savings—make some giant strides. Here is an example of how:

To make a rental-property investment, Lewis Newman purchases a single-family house in a blue-collar neighborhood for $50,000. He applies for a loan at his local bank, specifying that he will pay $20,000 down and that he would like a $30,000, 25-year mortgage. The loan is approved at an annual interest rate of 12 percent, and the monthly mortgage payment is $330.

Newman finds a family interested in the home and sets the monthly rent at $330, thus equaling the mortgage payment. (This is a typical situation since rental property of this type often produces little more than the mortgage payment, and equalizing the two is a safe assumption when planning such an investment.) Newman regretfully realizes that he will pay the other expenses out-of-pocket: $1,000 in property taxes, $400 for insurance, and $500 for repair and maintenance costs. This means that at the end of the year, he will have spent $1,900 more on the property than the $3,960 he received in rental income.

Newman then considers his tax situation. In this area, indeed, his gain is clear.

He deducts the interest he has paid as part of the mortgage

payment each month: $3,600 the first year (12 percent of $30,000, the amount of the loan).

He deducts the local real estate taxes ($1,000) and expenses for insurance, repairs and maintenance (a total of $900).

He deducts for depreciation of the house, as the tax law permits (on the theory that the property will decline in value from year to year as a rental unit). The amount he deducts in the first year for depreciation is $6,000, which is 12 percent of the cost of the property. This deduction is a decided advantage to the owner and is about *triple* the deduction that would have been taken under the tax law prior to 1981. (An explanation of the new depreciation rules follows.)

Together, these tax write-offs provide Newman with a total tax deduction of $11,500 for the first year he owns the rental property. In effect, this deduction from income reduces Newman's taxes by almost $4,500 (assuming a salary of $40,000 and a 1982 tax bracket of 39 percent, on a joint tax return). This erases the cash deficit of $1,900 on the house and produces an after-tax profit of $2,600.

What is more, Newman should be able to stay close to the $2,600 annual profit level each year during the early years of owning the property. Certainly, there are complications. Some tax deductions—such as depreciation and interest—will decrease over time. Also, the owner may have problems with the IRS if he shows a tax loss on the property year after year—that is, large tax deductions used to offset other taxable income.

But on the plus side, the amount Newman charges for rent should increase, assuming inflation remains with us. (In the past 10 years, rental rates have risen as much as 100 percent in many urban neighborhoods.) Moreover, Newman—if he is like a large percentage of owners of residential rental property—will see the value of his investment increase year to year. Like rents, property values of low-cost rental houses have risen as much as 100 percent since 1970. *And note:* Lower tax rates under the new law will help Newman when one day he sells the house at a profit.

Newman's example points especially to the principal advantage realized by real estate investors under the new tax law: improved depreciation rules. These regulations apply to any investment in real estate—a factory, warehouse, store building, or rental houses, apartments, or condominiums. The rules are effective for property purchased after January 1, 1981, and thus apply to your tax filing in April 1982. The major change is that cost recovery—depreciation—can be completed over a 15-year period. This means that you may deduct from your taxable income each year for 15 years a portion of the cost of the property you purchased. At the end of 15 years, you will have subtracted the total cost of the real estate. Under the old law, depreciation terms ran from 25 years to as long as 40 years, depending on the type of business real estate (industrial, commercial or rental.) What happens when you sell property at or before the end of the 15-year period is discussed below.

Write-Off Methods

Two mechanisms for depreciating real estate are provided by the Economic Recovery Tax Act:
- The straight-line method, and
- The Accelerated Cost Recovery System method (ACRS).

Straight-line depreciation is the easiest. You simply divide the cost of the property by 15 (the minimum number of years for writing off property). You then deduct 1/15th from your taxable income each year—as if it were an expense—until you have written off the total cost of the property. For example: Suppose that in 1982 you purchase a small, four-unit building for $150,000. Divide that amount by 15 and you get $10,000. That is the amount you deduct annually for the allowable minimum 15-year period using the straight-line method. Under the new law you can depreciate property over a time period as long as 45 years, using the straight-line method. That would produce an annual deduction of $3,333 per year for a $150,000 property. This might serve a purpose where an investor wanted to spread out tax deductions over many years. Most investors, however, will want to make use of the 15-year depreciation write-off, which produces large early deductions.

The second depreciation method, ACRS, uses the 15-year write-off and sets the percentage of the property's cost you are permitted to deduct annually in a table provided by the U.S. Treasury Department. The write-off or annual tax deduction is "accelerated" in the early years, thus producing large deductions.

The Treasury table is given in figure 5-1.

FIGURE 5-1

Year of the Tax Deduction	Percentage of the Cost Deductible for the Year Based on the Month the Property Is Placed in Service											
	Jan	Feb	Mar	Apr	May	June	July	Aug	Sep	Oct	Nov	Dec
1	12*	11	10	9	8	7	6	5	4	3	2	1
2	10	10	11	11	11	11	11	11	11	11	11	12
3	9	9	9	9	10	10	10	10	10	10	10	10
4	8	8	8	8	8	8	9	9	9	9	9	9
5	7	7	7	7	7	7	8	8	8	8	8	8
6	6	6	6	6	7	7	7	7	7	7	7	7
7	6	6	6	6	6	6	6	6	6	6	6	6
8	6	6	6	6	6	6	6	6	6	6	6	6
9	6	6	6	6	6	6	6	6	6	6	6	6
10	6	6	6	6	6	6	6	6	6	6	6	6
11	6	6	6	6	6	6	6	6	6	6	6	6
12	6	6	6	6	6	6	6	6	6	6	6	6
13	6	6	6	6	6	6	6	6	6	6	6	6
14	6	6	6	6	6	6	6	6	6	6	6	6
15	5	5	5	5	5	5	5	5	5	5	5	5

* 11.66 percent rounded to 12 percent.

To use this table, you begin with the month you placed your property in service, meaning date of first rental. For example, if the building was put into service in January, you may deduct the maximum allowable amount for the first year—

11.66 percent of the cost (rounded in the table to 12 percent). If the beginning date is December, you are permitted to deduct only 1/12th of the annual allowable amount, or one percent of the cost, for that year.

The prime advantage of ACRS is that it allows you to deduct larger amounts in the early years of ownership. Still, it spreads the deductions over a 15-year period, with the total cost being deducted by the end of the fifteenth year. This 15-year period is mandatory. You may *not* choose a longer depreciation timetable unless you use the simpler straight-line method.

Deciding which method of depreciation to use may be difficult, and you may want to seek advice from a tax specialist. You can make rough comparisons, though, using the information provided here. As an example, suppose you purchased and placed into service a small apartment building in January of this year. The investment was $150,000.

• Using the straight-line method—as explained above—you would divide the cost of the property, $150,000 by 15, the minimum number of years over which the property may be written off. The figure you arrive at is $10,000, and that is the amount you may deduct each year.

• Using the Accelerated Cost Recovery System, the amount you deduct is dependent upon the figures provided in the chart. Locate the January column. Under it, you will find that you may deduct 12 percent of cost the first year, 10 percent the second, and so on. This means that you could deduct $18,000 the first year of ownership, $15,000 the second, and decreasing amounts each year after that, until you have written off 100 percent at the end of 15 years.

Whether it is better for you to deduct an equal amount each year for the full 15 years or more in the early period of ownership depends on your tax situation. Some people with high incomes prefer to take the maximum (ACRS) amount allowable, assuming that in later years they will have other tax deductions to improve their tax situation. Other investors fear the tax consequences upon sale of the property. We will examine this issue next.

Selling Investment Property

Greater tax advantages are effective under the new law during the time you *own* investment real estate, *and* when you sell. For example:

Investors, like homeowners, profit from the reduction in the capital gains tax rate, explained in chapter 8. If you sell property after holding it for more than a year, you pay a maximum tax of 20 percent on the profit, assuming you are in the new maximum 50 percent tax bracket.

Another part of the Economic Recovery Tax Act affecting real estate sales is the section on "recapture" rules. These regulations are used by the Internal Revenue Service to take back or recapture some of the earlier advantages of depreciation deductions, when eventually you sell your investment property. IRS accomplishes its recapture by taxing the profit you make on the sale. How taxation is applied depends upon the type of property:

• If you own residential investment property, like most small investors in real estate, a percentage of your profit on a sale may be subject to your high, ordinary tax rate. This amount would represent any depreciation deductions taken under the accelerated ACRS formula. The straight-line method, in effect, produces only a low-rate capital gains tax. The lesson here is that you probably should use the straight-line depreciation method to avoid paying higher taxes at the time you sell.

• If you own commercial or industrial property, the entire amount you deduct as depreciation under the accelerated ACRS method will be taxed at the higher rate. However, if you depreciate the property using only the straight-line method, you entirely avoid being taxed at your high ordinary rate. You have only the lower capital gains tax to contend with.

Here is an example showing what this means:

Lewis Newman, who purchased the rental house for $50,000, holds the property for 10 years. He sells it and receives a check for $100,000, the amount remaining after the real estate agent's fee and a number of minor expenses are paid. From that $100,000, he pays the bank $26,000, the balance due on the mortgage on the property (most of the early payments covered the interest due). This leaves him with $74,000 to deposit in the bank or to invest. To the IRS, though, his profit is $50,000—the difference between the amount he paid for the house and the *net* amount he received when he sold it.

Complicating the sale is Newman's use of the ACRS depreciation method. During the full 10 years he owned the property, he deducted $38,000 in depreciation. If he had used the straight-line method, he would have deducted only $33,300 in depreciation. Under the new tax law, Newman must pay a tax on the difference between his depreciation deductions using the accelerated method and the amount he would have deducted using the straight-line method. This difference is $4,700 ($38,000 minus $33,300).

The rate of tax Newman pays on this $4,700 is his top marginal tax rate. In this case, he owes a tax of $1,551, or 33 percent—a tax bracket lower than his current 1982 bracket of 43 percent, under the new tax law.

Newman also must pay capital gains taxes on the remainder of his gain—$45,300. This figure is arrived at by subtracting $4,700 from his $50,000 profit on the sale. Newman, having paid his penalty tax for using accelerated depreciation, pays the capital gains rate on the rest since he held the property in excess of the minimum one-year requirement. His capital gains tax is 40 percent times $45,300 times 33 percent, or $5,980.

His total tax liability on the sale of the house is $7,531

($1,551 plus $5,980). This amount is less than the $8,600 that would have been due under prior law. Why? First, Newman's marginal tax bracket under the past tax law would have been spread over 30 years, permitting him an annual deduction of just $1,666 ($50,000—the cost of the property—divided by 30). The total amount of depreciation deductible during the 10 years he owned the property would have been $16,666, considerably less than the $33,000 under the new straight-line method or the $38,000 allowed using the ACRS formula.

The net effect: a tax saving under the new law of over $1,000 in cash, upon sale of the property. In addition, the tax deductions for depreciation over the 10 years of ownership, using the *straight-line formula,* entailing no tax recapture, would have been *$16,660* under the old law—and *$33,300* under the new law. To the real estate investor, these deductions are money in the bank.

Thus, the new law provides the real estate investor with substantial year-to-year cash advantages in the form of high tax deductions and a more favorable result upon final sale of property.

A New Tax Credit

The Economic Recovery Tax Act alters and increases the tax credit for persons who "rehabilitate" certain aging nonresidential commercial structures. For instance, a small investor upgrading an old warehouse into offices would qualify for the credit. So would someone who buys an aging store and remodels it into an antique shop or coffee house. Remember: A tax credit is more valuable than a tax deduction, since a credit is deducted from the tax you owe the Treasury. A deduction merely reduces your taxable income, and saves you less money—dollar for dollar—than a credit.

A similar tax credit for "rehab" of nonresidential business realty was provided under the old law. It was 10 percent of your costs of rehabilitating buildings at least 20 years old. This law expired on December 31, 1981.

The New Economic Recovery Tax Act provides a tax credit of:

• 15 percent of the cost of rehabilitating structures 30 years or older.

• 20 percent of the cost of rehabilitating those 40 years or older, and

• 25 percent of the cost of rehabilitating a "certified" historic structure. (Members of your local historical society should be able to help you find out if your building is certified or could be certified.)

What this means in dollar terms is this: If you spend $10,000 renovating a nonresidential building, you may subtract from your annual tax bill:

• $1,500 (15 percent of $10,000) if the building is 30 years old or more.

• $2,000 (20 percent of $10,000) if the building is 40 years old or older.

• $2,500 (25 percent of $10,000) if the building is a certified historic structure.

There is one catch. The IRS sets a minimum amount you must spend on rehabilitation to qualify for the tax credit. This amount is $5,000 *or* the "adjusted cost basis" of the property, whichever is greater. The adjusted cost basis is usually what you pay for the structure. For instance, if you pay $50,000 for a building over 40 years old, your tax basis is $50,000. Since your tax basis—$50,000—is greater than $5,000, you must spend at least $50,000 fixing up the building to qualify for the rehabilitation tax credit.

If you have owned the property for some years and depreciated a portion of it, the adjusted cost basis will be computed differently. An example: You purchased a building 30 years ago for $50,000. Using prior tax laws, you have depreciated it until its value is now listed on paper at $12,500. This figure is your adjusted cost basis. To qualify for the rehabilitation tax credit, you must spend at least $12,500 for rehabilitation. Usually, the new law favors a present owner of an old building who has owned it for many years.

A warning about making use of this tax credit: Be sure you can prove to the Internal Revenue Service that you have *rehabilitated* a structure, not simply performed a number of repairs. The most convincing evidence of rehabilitation is a set of architectural or engineering plans, outlining the renovation or restoration project. The combination of "rehab" tax credits and a 15-year depreciation write-off can produce some big tax benefits.

A Final Note

Comparing the tax advantages of potential real estate investments is complex but worthwhile. If you are considering buying or selling property, use the information available to you. Look at the costs and the advantages realistically. Ask yourself if the neighborhood will be good for rental property in five years, or 10 years. Ask yourself if the structure will need major repairs, and, if so, how much they will cost. Ask yourself if the local economy is withering and, if it is, will tenants be in short supply. Ask yourself if insurance costs could explode and if property taxes are expected to climb. Finding the answers is not too difficult and yet *many* small investors plunge in blindly.

Chapter 6

Planning to Retire in Comfort

Starting in 1982, many millions of taxpayers will be able to establish Individual Retirement Accounts (IRAs) even though they are covered by company pension plans or other Treasury qualified plans. Before this, employees with pension coverage were ineligible for personal IRAs. This is a momentus change in the law and is especially important in view of the evident weaknesses in the social security system which may result in a curtailment in social security payments in the future.

The Economic Recovery Tax Act, in fact, seems to have been adopted with just this sort of pattern in mind: less reliance on government-provided retirement benefits and more reliance on private planning and personal initiative. We—all of us—are being urged to plan ahead for retirement, with some favorable government tax rules as an aid. The new law outlines this approach and provides tax breaks for those who create and contribute to self-financed retirement plans. There is even a strong suggestion in the new law that we not rely too heavily on corporate pension, profit-sharing, and other types of retirement plans—or at least that we not rely solely on such plans. And this is, of course, entirely in line with the Reagan Administration's supply-side economics, which, in part, says that nearly everyone in the society should become more self-reliant.

The two principal types of retirement plans that are liberalized by the new law are the IRAs and Keogh plans, sometimes called HR 10 plans. (HR 10 is the number of the House of Representatives tax bill that created Keogh plans, while Vincent Keogh was the New York congressman who wrote the law.) The main difference between the plans is that while IRAs are designed for persons who work as employees, Keogh plans are structured for those who are self-employed: professionals, owners of small businesses, and such. Yet whether the new, liberal tax incentives will actually have the desired effect on American society is open to question. Keogh plans have been widely used in the past, possibly because self-employed people have been made quite aware of their many advantages. But IRAs—available under the old law on a more restricted basis than now—have recorded only minimal participation. The Treasury Department estimates that through mid-1981 only about 3 million of the 50 million eligible workers (those not covered by company pension or similar plans) have opened retirement accounts using the IRA format.

Proponents of the IRA concept (and in Washington the support is extensive and bipartisan) claim that this lack of popularity might be blamed on a lack of understanding, poor media coverage, and the fact, they say, that most people lack the determination needed to salt money away regularly for use in the distant future. This seems unlikely, especially since banks, insurance companies, and other sellers of formalized IRA plans have spent millions of dollars advertising them. The shortage of IRA customers, so to speak, might better be explained by the fact that most people find it difficult to part with even small portions of their paychecks—given the current high level of inflation and taxation. Surveys show that the great majority of eligible people *not* covered by IRAs before 1982 had incomes below $30,000 a year, and most of these had incomes below $20,000.

Understanding Individual Retirement Accounts

An IRA is basically a simple plan, authorized by the government and created by the taxpayer—using rules enforced by the Internal Revenue Service—to shelter funds until retirement. The beauty part is that (starting in 1982) you can put away up to $2,000 a year, as an individual, and let the money build up tax-free until the time you retire. (Under the old law, the limit was $1,500.) The funds are then paid out as taxable income—year to year, in most cases—but are taxable in the presumably lower brackets of one's retirement years. The investment advantage at the start is impressive. You may channel the money in many ways, and you have almost the full scope of investments at your disposal:

• Long-term bank deposits and certificates of deposit in banks paying high rates of interest, often 10 percent or more at this writing.

• Insurance company plans, mainly annuities that build up tax-free and pay out as you direct upon your retirement from the company. Interest rates are more modest: currently below the highest bank rates, although there are insurance features attached.

• Money market (mutual) funds that have been yielding 15 percent or more per year, of late—far and away the most popular form of noninsured investment since 1976.

• Mutual funds of all types, including those that are "safe" (portfolios invested solely in highest-quality bonds), those that are "balanced" (invested in a mix of stocks and bonds), and those that are riskier (invested in stocks of all kinds).

• Stocks, including individual issues (best if dividends are reinvested, which preserves the year-to-year tax-free feature of an IRA).

• *A combination* of these, as you choose.

Remember that the money deposited or "contributed" to

your IRA each year (up to the allowed amount) remains tax-free from year to year as it generates earnings. If you get a cash pay-out, however, you have taxable income. It is only accumulated earnings that are tax-free. Thus it is wise to invest in the vehicles in a way that produces a growth in values but without cash flow, year to year. In the case of stocks (above), for example, dividends that are automatically reinvested serve best for an IRA.

And just as a cash pay-out produces taxable income, an early withdrawal of funds from your account produces taxable income. You pay tax on the amount withdrawn at your ordinary tax rate, and, in addition, must pay *10 percent* of the money withdrawn early from the account—quite a penalty, indeed. "Early withdrawal," in the tax law, means a withdrawal at any time before the owner of the account reaches age 59½.

Yet the great flexibility of the IRA—with its new $2,000 limit and other dollar liberalizations—adds investment appeal. You may accept as the manager of your IRA the institution where the account is placed: the bank, savings and loan company, the insurance company, or such. If you do so, you would also accept whatever rate of return was earned by the institution. However, you may avoid being tied in, if you wish. You can manage your account yourself, placing the investments as you see fit, and use a bank, for example, merely as custodian of your IRA. The account, in any case, must be designated as an IRA, and this fulfills the formal requirements of the government and ensures that you will be eligible for the tax benefits.

Possibly the greatest flexibility lies in the fact that the owner of an IRA can switch investments as deemed necessary, though not more often than once a year. Moreover, there is no tax penalty for switching. You might change from a mutual fund to a single stock, or from a bank deposit to a money market fund, for example, and be able to do so without risking problems with the Internal Revenue Service. The danger, however, is that you might incur a penalty enforced by the bank or other institution: a loss of interest for a three-month period, or similar penalty. In some cases, when you switch investments under an IRA plan, the interest rate on the entire account may drop to the lowest legal rate allowed: 6 percent, say, in the case of savings banks and saving and loan companies.

The Old Law Versus the New

Under the old law, effective through 1981, annual IRA contributions were tax deductible up to $1,500 a year or 15 percent of the taxpayer's income, whichever was less. If you established a joint IRA for yourself and your spouse who did not work outside the home as an employee, the yearly tax-deductible contribution could have been as much as $1,750 or 15 percent, whichever was less.

If both you and your wife, or husband, held jobs as employees, and neither of you was covered by a company, union, or other group retirement plan, each of you could have established an IRA, and each could have contributed up to $1,500 or 15 percent of income. Note that an IRA could not have been established by a taxpayer already covered by a "qualified" retirement plan—meaning one that had been approved by the Internal Revenue Service in terms of the retirement tax advantages. IRAs could have been opened only by those who were employed but not covered by a qualified plan.

The Economic Recovery Tax Act liberalizes these rules and raises the ceilings for contributions to IRAs and other self-financed accounts. These are the changes:

• Individuals now may contribute *any* percentage (even 100 percent) of their pay up to a maximum contribution of $2,000 to an IRA. The strict 15 percent rule has been dropped. This is particularly helpful to a part-time worker who earns just a few thousand dollars each year. Such an individual can set aside $2,000 yearly, put it into an IRA, and let the money build tax-free. The rule is a boon to two-earner families. One example: Say that you are employed full-time. To help balance the family budget, your spouse takes a part-time job, working 20 hours a week and earning $100 each week, or $5,200 a year. Under the old law, your spouse could put only $780 (15 percent times $5,200) into a separate IRA. The new law raises the limit to $2,000—an increase of 156 percent. With two separate IRAs, the total IRA deduction for the family could be $4,000 a year.

• Not only may you open an IRA even if you are employed and covered by a Treasury-qualified pension or other retirement plan, but you may open an IRA if you are self-employed even though you are covered by a Keogh plan (explained later in this chapter).

• The ceiling for contributions to dual IRAs has been raised for married couples in families where only one spouse is employed. If you are personally eligible to contribute to an IRA—as an employee—you can maintain an account for yourself and also establish a separate "spousal" IRA for your nonemployed spouse. In such case, the maximum deductible contribution is limited to $2,250, for *both* accounts. This is not a joint account, but two separate IRAs, or one IRA with a "subaccount," totaling no more than $2,250 in contributions for the year. This is a very simple question of filling out the right form at a bank or other financial institution—part of the easy formality of setting up IRAs.

Here are three examples that help illustrate the above rules:

• Gary McMann is single, earns a salary of $6,000 a year, and is not covered by any approved pension, profit-sharing, or other company retirement plan. Under the old law, he could exclude from taxable income $900 (15 percent times $6,000) by placing the money in an IRA. The new law permits him to exclude $2,000.

• Max Schultz is married, earns $50,000 a year, and is covered by his company's qualified pension plan. His wife,

Betty, earns $3,000 a year from a part-time job and has no pension or other retirement plan coverage. Under the old law, the couple could put $450 (15 percent times $3,000) into an IRA, based on Mrs. Schultz's annual earnings. Under the new law, the couple could establish two IRAs and each year put $2,000 in each, deducting $4,000 from their taxable income.

• Sam Block is married, earns $50,000 a year, and is enrolled in his company's Treasury-qualified retirement program providing a pension and deferred pay (a percentage of salary put aside, or deferred, to become payable in retirement). Edna, his wife, is not employed outside the home and consequently is not covered by any type of retirement plan. The old law held the couple to the limits of Sam Block's company retirement program. Under the new law, they may create two spousal IRAs, deposit as much as $2,250 total each year, and deduct that amount from taxable income.

Capturing IRA Deductions by Using Company Plans

Suppose that you are covered by a qualified retirement plan at work but still want to capture the extra $2,000 IRA deduction permitted under the new tax law. However, you would prefer to use a company plan as a conduit for your IRA funds. That is, you want to contribute voluntarily to a company-sponsored retirement plan rather than establish a separate IRA on your own. You might feel, for example, that the company plan is well managed and that the accumulated earnings of the fund would be better than you could manage by investing yourself. The Economic Recovery Tax Act allows you to do just this. You can deduct from taxable income your voluntary contributions to a Treasury-qualified group account managed by your employer: a pension fund, profit-sharing account, or—if it should apply to your employment—a Keogh plan. This is a major reversal in the law, of course, since in the past employees covered by company plans were not permitted to establish IRAs or deduct voluntary contributions.

Keep in mind, however, that this deduction is limited to the new IRA ceiling of $2,000 annually, and remember that if you choose to voluntarily contribute to a company plan—assuming the company offers this privilege, of course—you cannot set up a separate IRA apart from the company plan. Also note that amounts contributed by you and deducted from salary or wages by the company cannot be withdrawn prior to your reaching age 59½ *without a penalty*. This penalty parallels the penalty for early withdrawal from an IRA: the amount prematurely taken from the account becomes taxable, and in addition, 10 percent of this amount is payable to the Internal Revenue Service.

Another important point is that voluntary contributions to any employer-sponsored retirement plan (in this case, in lieu of an independent IRA), as well as payouts from IRAs and Keogh plans, are not covered by the Treasury's special 10-year averaging rule which applies to lump-sum withdrawals at the time of retirement. When conventional pension or other payouts are withdrawn from the account all at once, instead of being taxed on the entire sum in the years withdrawn, the lump sum is subject to tax averaging over 10 years. This is a considerable break, since the applicable tax bracket is much lower than it would be otherwise. But note: Although this beneficial 10-year averaging formula cannot be applied to an employee's IRA contributions, the taxpayer can use the general income-averaging rules of the tax law which are intended to help people whose incomes advance rapidly in a short span of time. This formula is highly complex and should never be applied without professional advice.

A number of companies use a retirement account known as a Simplified Employee Pension (SEP) rather than conventional structured corporate pension plans or similar plans. A SEP is a streamlined company fund to which both employee and employer may contribute. The employee must include in his taxable income any contribution to the plan made by the employer, but at the same time he is permitted to take an **offsetting tax deduction from his income.** If the taxpayer contributes to the SEP personally, he obtains a tax deduction for the contribution. The company's contribution to the SEP is subject to the same limit which applies to contributions by self-employed persons to Keogh plans. The employee's contribution is limited by the IRA ceiling.

Just as the new tax law increases both IRA and Keogh annual contributions limits, it similarly raises the limits under the SEP plans. Thus, the company's contribution level goes from 15 percent of the employee's earnings with a maximum contribution of $7,500 per year (in 1981) to 15 percent of earnings with a maximum of $15,000 (in 1982). The employee's individual contribution goes from $1,500 to $2,000. Even if your employer contributes the maximum $15,000 to the SEP, **you still may funnel up to $2,000 into the account, within the IRA limit, and deduct the amount from your taxable income.**

The Internal Revenue Service does not treat contributions made to a retirement account by an employer as part of the individual's earnings, as long as the maximum levels are observed. Questions about any company plans involving IRA contributions ought to be checked with the company employee benefits department before an investment is made in an independent IRA.

Special IRA Provisions and Restrictions

Divorced couples are given special attention in the new law governing IRAs. In brief, the law provides relief for a nonworking divorced spouse whose former marriage partner had contributed to a spousal IRA during three of the five years prior to the divorce. When this requirement is met, the nonworking divorced spouse may contribute to an IRA and deduct annually up to $1,125, even if he or she remarries. The top limit of $1,125 is 50 percent of the new maximum contribution ($2,250) to a spousal IRA. The idea is to afford nonworking divorced spouses a chance to build an IRA fund—a breach of the general rule that the owner of an IRA must be employed.

Here is an example: Mary Smith is 45 years old, and over the 5 previous years her husband contributed to a spousal IRA for Mary's benefit. She and her husband are then divorced, and although Mary is not employed away from home, she contributes $500 a year to her spousal IRA. That this is permitted by the new law is important to Mary Smith. If Mary's contributed funds earn 10 percent annually, and the earnings are compounded in the account, she will have a nest egg of over $28,500 at age 65—20 years later. One note: If Mary had taken a part-time job and earned only $2,000 a year, she could—under the new law—have contributed that entire amount to her own retirement fund—tax-free.

As explained earlier, the money your account builds year-to-year may be drawn out beginning at age 59½, without penalty. Moreover, the IRA must be drawn against by age 70½, and such payments must be at least as much as would be due if the funds were paid out on an annuity basis over your remaining life expectancy. The idea, of course, is to prevent use of IRAs to shelter funds from taxes, apart from retirement needs, although some fine points of this rule have never been made clear. If you do not start receiving an adequate distribution of the money by age 70½, a penalty tax of 50 percent is assessed against the difference between the payout that should have been received and the amount actually received.

The penalty rule is harsh but is not followed to the letter of the law. If you can show that you made a "reasonable error," or were misled by an investment advisor, or such, the Internal Revenue Service may waive the penalty.

There are other restrictions placed on IRAs by the new law. For example, while the law permits almost complete freedom in investing IRA funds, it makes one major exception. You may not invest in arts, antiques, coins, stamps, or other collectibles. The old law was more liberal on this point, permitting such investments. The new law, however, clamps down and treats investments in collectibles as withdrawals from the account. The heavy "early withdrawal" penalty is imposed: The value of the collectibles—determined by an approved appraiser, if necessary—becomes taxable income to the owner of the IRA, and 10 percent of that value is tacked on as an added penalty. Moreover, taxpayers who invest in collectibles using IRA funds are prohibited from adding new funds to their retirement accounts for a period of five years.

As might be expected, these penalties have prompted some angry reactions. Many taxpayers, indeed, feel that they are highly skilled at collectibles investments and resent being denied this vehicle in placing their IRA funds. The reason Congress has taken this action is explained in a report by the House Ways and Means Committee, which writes tax legislation. It says, in a word, that the Committee was "concerned" that collectibles divert retirement savings from "thrift institutions and other traditional investment media." Thus, the ban on collectibles might have been a means of boosting the fortunes of the sagging savings banks and the saving and loan industry. At this writing, there is some sentiment in Congress in favor of abolishing the anti-collectibles rule.

"Rolling Over" Your IRA Funds

Under the new law, like the old, taxpayers are permitted to "roll over" IRA and company pension funds from one retirement plan to another—without being penalized by the IRS. This, of course, is a boon to people who change jobs. You transfer your IRA contributions or other pension funds from your previous employer's Treasury-qualified plan to your new employer's plan. The changeover is a mere formality. The rollover also is helpful to people seeking higher returns on their IRA investments. For example, you may be unhappy with the 3 percent return on your IRA annuity policy, and—as you are permitted to do—cancel the policy in favor of an IRA money market account, or such, paying a substantially higher interest rate.

Thus, great freedom is allowed for you to switch between two company retirement plans or change investment vehicles, and IRAs are specifically covered by these liberal rules. There are two keys, however, to rollovers between company plans. One is that the two plans must be "qualified" by the Treasury as bona fide pension or other retirement plans, or as Individual Retirement Accounts. In most cases, this is a formality, but sometimes a company plan will not be "qualified" because it does not meet certain federal requirements. (For example, it might discriminate in favor of a limited class of company employees.) The other requirement involves timing. The rule is that you must finalize the rollover within 60 days, or the money you receive as a lump-sum payout from your old plan will be treated as taxable income.

Here is an example:

Justin Miller works for a financial services firm. In June of 1982 he resigns and joins another company. In late July he receives a check for $6,000—the cash value of his retirement account with his former employer. Upon receiving the check, he informs his new company that he wants to deposit the $6,000 in its retirement fund. The firm has a policy of approving such transfers into its own account (under the law, it could refuse) and adds Miller's money to an individual account in his name in its general pension plan. At the end of the tax year, Miller is not penalized by the IRS, since he completed the rollover of his cash payout within the specified 60-day time limit.

Had Miller been unable to find a new job within 60 days, he could have set up a temporary IRA at a bank or other investment institution—thus covering the time gap. He could then close this account in favor of a new employer's retirement fund at a later date—and without breaking the continuity of his IRA account.

Understanding Keogh Plans

Keogh plans are founded on the proposition that self-employed people should have the right to set aside—tax-free—a reasonable percentage of their income for retirement years. By definition, a Keogh plan is quite similar to an IRA. Indeed, like the IRA, the Keogh top limit for yearly contributions has been raised by the new law. The deduction limit is increased to 15 percent of the self-employed person's yearly earnings to a maximum of $15,000. This doubles the pre-1982 top limit of $7,500.

Both types of plans are designed to operate under Treasury rules for the purpose of sheltering some income from taxes and letting it build tax-free until retirement. Moreover, a Keogh plan, like an IRA, may include certificates of deposit, stocks, bonds, money market shares, or other investments, and may be established at a bank or insurance company or any traditional financial institution. If the plan, or fund, is formally established as a Keogh plan, the money may be managed by the company that serves as custodian or by the owner of the account. Usually, however, self-employed people choose to let the fund be managed by the custodian company.

The money or securities held in the account remain tax-free from year to year, and this also is true of any gains or returns on the principal, assuming this income accumulates within the account. If it is paid out year to year, it is taxed year to year. Generally, however, no taxes are paid until the money is drawn out in retirement years. Then, as in the case of IRA accounts, taxation is at the ordinary tax rate of the individual—but probably, in a tax bracket that is considerably below the bracket of the individual's final earning years.

A catch to Keogh plans is that if the self-employed taxpayer, in turn, has employees, the taxpayer must include them in the Keogh plan—if they have three years or more of service. Cash contributions must then be made, and this obligation sometimes prompts self-employed people to decide against establishing a Keogh retirement program. Might some other form of investment serve me better? they ask. Generally, only an investment that would return a high yield—possibly 15 percent, or more, in today's high-interest market—could beat the advantages of a tax-favored Keogh plan, even with the burden of making employee contributions.

A great temptation to owners of Keogh plans is to dip into the funds to help pay for a new car or a trip to Europe or a daughter's wedding. But you cannot withdraw money by "borrowing" from your own Keogh plan without interfering with the tax-free treatment of the plan.

For years, the rule has been that Keogh plans may not make loans to owner-employees or to anyone who owns more than a 10 percent interest in the business, as in a partnership, and who consequently holds more than a 10 percent interest in the retirement program. To the U.S. Treasury, permitting this type of borrowing would be to extend an unjustified benefit. It would cheat the IRS of taxes by allowing a tax deduction (the Keogh annual deduction) covering money that was later used for some purpose that was not intended by the deduction. Thus, the old law—and the new tax law, as well—have prohibited this type of self-dealing.

The new law goes a step ahead and makes the rule harder. The no-borrowing rule now includes *all* partners in a business having a Keogh plan, even though they may own less than a 10 percent interest. Further, no partner may pledge his interest in the Keogh account to make a loan—and still retain the Keogh tax advantages. The new rule became effective for loans made, renewed, or negotiated after Dec. 31, 1981. What happens if you disregard the rule and borrow from your Keogh plan? As you might expect, the amount of the "loan" will be treated as a "distribution"—meaning taxable income.

If you are wondering how the IRS learns of such borrowing, remember that both Keogh plans and IRAs are not just ordinary bank accounts. They are accounts set up under special rules, one of these being that the custodian or trustee (usually a financial company) is required to inform the IRS, via information reports, if and when you abuse the concept. Just as a bank sends a routine information report to the IRS showing the interest paid on an account, it also must send similar reports on IRAs and Keogh plans. Whether the IRS will take notice of your loans and enforce the rule on borrowing, is open to question. The wise course is to play it safe. Assume that it will.

Another temptation for Keogh plan owners is padding the account. This means that you put more money into the account than is permitted under the 15 percent rule, hoping that the extra funds will creep under the tax-shelter umbrella of the plan. Under the old law, contributions to a Keogh plan over the allowable limit were subject to a 6 percent penalty on the excess. In addition, of course, the excess money became taxable. The new law provides a little leeway: Excess contributions to a Keogh fund by an owner-employee still are subject to a 6 percent penalty—but the penalty is waived if (1) the person making the contribution does not take a tax deduction covering the excess amount, and (2) the excess amount—along with any earnings that it generates—is withdrawn from the account before the due date of the owner-employee's personal tax return (April 15). The law has no parallel rule on excess IRA contributions.

Some Keogh Restrictions

Remember that the rule on the investment of Keogh moneys is liberal. Most financial investments are permitted. Indeed, real estate investing is expected to become more important to owners of Keogh plans whose contributions to the fund can reach as high as $15,000 a year. You put, say, $10,000 a year into the mortgage payments on a highly valued parcel of raw land, expecting great appreciation. Still, there is one limitation built into the new law covering Keogh management: The IRA restriction on art, antiques, and other collectibles extends to Keogh plans. (The law even mentions "alcoholic beverages" as one of the prohibited items, since some IRA and Keogh investors have put money into rare wines.) Moreover, the new law gives the Treasury the authority to expand the list of prohibited investments for both Keogh and IRA owners. It limits the list to collectibles, however. Generally, it has been the Keogh investor—with a greater amount of money available—who has gone into such exotica as vintage wines and classic automobiles.

What happens if you have a Keogh plan and divert funds into collectibles? This happens: Their value—as in the case of IRAs—is treated as a distribution from the fund, meaning that it becomes fully taxable income. In addition, a penalty of 10 percent of value is imposed.

One happy note: The rule banning collectibles may be abolished by Congress one day. If IRA investors are upset about the rule (as they are), Keogh investors are even more annoyed, since their retirement funds are much bigger and can be more successfully channeled into collectibles such as coins and stamps, which have been especially popular with investors.

Again, remember that establishing an IRA or a Keogh plan is an uncomplicated procedure, as noted earlier. You needn't even have the approval of the Internal Revenue Service. One note about this fast formality: You may be asked by the financial institution in which you invest if you wish to provide for survivorship rights for your spouse or children. It is a point to think about in advance.

Chapter **7** _____

The New Incentive Stock Option

For high-salaried business executives perhaps the biggest boon in the new tax law is a device known as the "incentive stock option"—ISO for short. It has such fine built-in tax advantages that some executives may find it to be more beneficial to them than even the reduction of the capital gains tax rate to a maximum of 20 percent (see chapter 7). The option, in a word, is a preferred method by which an executive can own shares in his or her employer company at a bare minimum cost in taxes. The reason for providing such breaks as the ISO to the country's affluent executive group is that such laws are part of the Reagan Administration's trickle-down theory: If the managers of business and industry prosper, so will the businesses—and so will all the employees. Indeed, the ISO is a way of luring executives into better performance for the corporation and its stockholders. In any case, the details of the ISO require close scrutiny.

What Are Incentive Stock Options?

The incentive stock option is a company-created device that gives an executive the right to purchase a specific number of shares in the company employing the executive—at a specific price and within a specific time-frame. The option is granted by the company on a certain date, and the executive can immediately exercise the option—that is, purchase the shares—or wait until a later time when, he hopes, the price of the shares will be higher. If he exercises the option two or three years later, the option allows him to purchase the stock at the "option price": what it was selling for at the time the option was granted.

For instance, suppose you were granted an option to buy 1,000 shares of your company's stock on January 10, 1982, when the shares were selling for $20 each. You exercise (buy the shares) on February 1, 1983, by which time the price has climbed to $25 a share. With an incentive stock option, you purchase the 1,000 shares at $20 each—the option price—and have an immediate profit on paper of $5,000.

You pay no tax at the time of purchase—one of the beauty parts of the ISO. The $5,000 profit rides tax-free as long as you hold the shares. If you and other executives in the company perform on a high standard, and the company prospers, the shares may well go to an even higher price. If after another year or two you sell the shares at, say, $30, you have an overall profit of $10 per share ($30 less $20). Thus, your profit on the option transaction is $10,000. This profit is taxed in the year in which you sell the shares, but—and this is another big break— the tax is figured not at your income tax rate but at the lower capital gains tax rate. Thus, only 40 percent of the gain, or $4,000 in this case, is subject to income tax. For a high-salaried executive, in the 50 percent maximum tax bracket, this means a 20 percent tax on the $10,000—or a tax of $2,000.

In order to understand the new ISO clearly, it is necessary to look briefly at other types of options. Formerly, stock options took two forms: "qualified" (meaning they were approved by the Treasury according to certain liberal rules similar to the ISO rules), and "nonqualified" (meaning, in effect, taxable options).

THE NEW INCENTIVE STOCK OPTION

The qualified option was highly valued by executives for many years, until it was phased out of the law by a reform-minded Congress during the 1970s. In 1976, it was quashed entirely, and ceased to exist in terms of new options being exercised as of May 20, 1981.

The nonqualified option still exists and is used widely today in business and industry. When attention began to shift away from qualified options in 1976—because they were being phased out—corporations began to rely more heavily on the nonqualified option, which was not "tax-favored" and thus continued to be permitted by the law. Under this type of option, the executive pays ordinary income tax on his option profit at the time the option is exercised. (The tax break found in the old qualified option and in the new ISO—providing for *no* tax at the time of exercise—is not present in a nonqualified option.) The tax, of course, is levied on the difference between the original option price as of the date the option was granted and the price at the time of exercise—when the shares are bought by the executive. This difference is called the "option price spread." Note that the tax—under the nonqualified stock option—is at the ordinary income tax rate, not the preferred capital gains rate.

Thus, the nonqualified option is simply a promise by the company that the executive may purchase a specific number of company shares at a specific price—namely, the price at the time the option is granted. The executive's profit upon exercise, as explained above, is fully taxable at that time. When eventually the executive sells the shares, he is taxed on any *additional* profit at the lower capital gains tax rate, just as in the case of any investment. Meanwhile, the company that has granted the nonqualified option—since the option involves no special tax breaks for the recipient executive—gets a tax deduction in the amount of the original price spread. If the executive exercises the option for $20 a share at a time when the shares are worth $25, and he buys 1,000 shares, his $5,000 profit is taxable in his ordinary tax bracket and the company takes a tax deduction of $5,000. It is as if the company had paid the executive a $5,000 cash bonus.

Who Receives Incentive Stock Options?

Obviously the ISO gives the executive a much better tax result than does the nonqualified option. But since the executive who is granted an ISO pays no tax on his option spread at the time of exercise, his company—as might be expected—loses the tax deduction that is available to it under the nonqualified option plan.

In any case, the ISO was placed in the Economic Recovery Tax Act to pick up where the old defunct qualified option left off. The ISO was put into the new law to enable executives to share in the profitability of their companies—with tax lures to keep them attached to the companies. Precisely who will receive the coveted ISOs will no doubt vary. In some large companies the ISOs will probably go to a handful of top executives, while other companies will extend the list of recipients to middle management.

To many companies—despite the added cost—the ISOs present a logical and easy way to reward people. This is partly because the options do not show up in the company bookkeeping as salary costs. The accounting aspects of the options are complex, but suffice it to say that if you are a senior or middle manager and are changing companies in the foreseeable future, it may pay you to learn about the incentive stock options and how they work. And take note: If you are in a key position in a small or large family-controlled business, by all means bone up on the ISO. You may be able to apply it very profitably within your own company.

The latest information is that considerable numbers of executives are bargaining for incentive options upon joining new companies and many are gaining them as part of the total compensation package. In any case, you can't be a manager, executive, or savvy businessman or businesswoman and not be aware of the ins and outs of this benefit.

How the New Incentive Stock Options Are Taxed

To clarify the tax aspects of the ISOs, here is a review:

• The Internal Revenue Service recognizes no taxable gain to the executive on an ISO at the time the option is granted by the company.

• There is no taxable gain and thus no tax at the time the executive exercises an ISO. (It is only the nonqualified option that produces such a tax.)

• There is taxable income upon the eventual sale of ISO shares, but this tax is levied at the lower capital gains tax rate.

The above are the three basic taxation rules covering ISOs. In addition, there is a fourth rule that applies to a small percentage of taxpayers: The option price spread as of the time the shares are purchased under an ISO plan, does not become a "tax preference" item for those taxpayers who might be subject to the 15 percent minimum tax. The 15 percent minimum tax is assessed against those who—by taking advantage of various tax rules throughout the law—would otherwise pay little or no income tax despite high income. This fourth rule for ISOs means, in brief, that executives who gain a profit on an option price spread need not have this amount of money counted toward a possible 15 percent minimum tax—which is an "add-on" income tax for a relatively small number of taxpayers. The rule, inserted in the fine print of the new ISO law, is an important advantage even though it will affect only a few high-income individuals.

Other Rules Governing Incentive Options

There are several operational rules that govern ISOs. These are as follows:

THE NEW INCENTIVE STOCK OPTION

• Gains from the sale of ISO shares will be taxed as capital gains only if certain criteria are met. Specifically, an executive who exercises an option must own the shares for at least a full year. Moreover, he or she must not sell the shares until at least two years have passed since the date the option was granted (regardless of the date of purchase of the shares). Thus, if shares were granted on January 15, 1982, and bought by the executive on April 15, 1982, the executive would be required to hold the shares (as owner) until January 15, 1984—two years after the option was granted, even though the general rule for capital gains is one year. If he bought the shares at a later date, say in 1985, he would be required to hold them for only one year to gain the capital gains tax advantage.

Requiring the executive to hold the stock for at least one year after the date of exercise of an incentive option seems quite reasonable, when compared to the rules governing the now defunct qualified stock option. The holding period (or ownership period) for a qualified stock option was three years.

This, then, is another tax break built into the ISO law. As an investor, the executive, in owning shares in his own company, can now have a profit, and take it sooner—after just one year—without the possible risk of having to hold the shares for three years before selling. There is less downside risk: that is, less risk that the shares might decline in value at some later date. If the executive sells the shares in under one year (or in under two years after the date of granting of the option), he will be taxed at the high ordinary tax rate, thus losing the capital gains advantage.

• From the date the option is granted until three months before the date the option is exercised, the executive must be an employee of the company granting the option, or of a parent or subsidiary company, or of a company that has assumed responsibility for the option as a result of a corporate reorganization or merger.

This rule adds flexibility to the option law under certain

conditions. If you are on a company's list of optionees, you can actually leave the company, if you wish, and exercise the stock option within three months after departing, and still obtain the tax advantages. The condition is that the company agrees to the date of exercise—usually in an employment contract or arrangement made before the option is granted.

A further important point is that if your company is acquired by another firm, usually you will not lose your option rights. If you are considering joining a new company and stock options are in the picture, you will be wise to weigh this rule—assuming you are on a managerial or executive level. The rule makes ISOs more attractive, considering the great number of corporate mergers occurring each year.

A point on small, emerging companies: Note that the new entrepreneurial companies, oftentimes started on a lean budget, are among the most frequent users of the stock option. The indications at this writing are that many such firms, especially in high-technology, will use ISOs to lure talented people. The options will be offered to supplement modest cash salaries so that the enterprise can attract engineers, scientists, and others who normally would command much higher salaries. If you are such a person, by all means take special pains to study the fine print of the new stock option law.

• In the event of an executive's dismissal owing to disability, he or she has 12 months following termination of employment in which to exercise an ISO and still obtain the tax advantages. In the event of death, the beneficiaries of the optionee receive the full benefit of the option and—if it is unexercised—may exercise it within the original option term of years or as provided in the stock option plan.

• Incentive options must be granted by the management of the company within 10 years of the date the stock option plan is formally approved by the shareholders (usually accomplished at an annual meeting of shareholders). However, the management need not seek approval by the shareholders in order to modify an old option plan dating to past years—as in the case of a company that has a qualified option plan that was fully operative up until May 20, 1981.

Moreover, an incentive option must be exercised by the optionee within 10 years of the date the option is granted. Here again there is flexibility that did not exist under the old law governing qualified options. The previous law had a five-year limit. An executive can now receive his or her option and hold it—seeing what the stock does on the market—and not invest any cash until as many as 10 years have passed.

• The option price must equal or exceed the fair market value of the stock at the time the option is granted. A good faith attempt to value the stock accurately—in the case of a corporation whose stock is not actively traded—is deemed to satisfy this requirement. This rule means that an employer can't price the stock below the current market price or established value, thus giving the optionee a bigger option price spread. Rather, the bargaining point an executive faces will be over the number of shares optioned. That is the point of the option game.

Persons considering new management jobs—particularly in small, emerging companies—might wisely sacrifice some ready salary for an option and thus get a cut in the profits of the company. They might follow this scenario: Take $40,000 in salary plus an option on 10,000 shares of stock at the current price of $1 a share. Invest that $10,000 when the stock has risen to $3. They thereby acquire $30,000 in stock for a payment of $10,000 and pay no tax until they sell later. If they hold it for two or three years, they pay the capital gains rate (40 percent of gain taxable).

And these numbers can be increased considerably: The $1 stock might go to $10 in five years, and the employee will then have $100,000 in company shares at a cost of $10,000. Options are a very good bet if you have faith in your company—for example, a young high-tech company that holds some promising patents and is well managed.

Large established firms will have a fixed policy on options, and here potential employees must sell themselves as being worth a job that merits an option. Remember: Many large companies grant stock options to hundreds of upper-, middle-, and lower-ranking managers.

Using Stock to Buy More Stock

There is one very potent clause in the new ISO law that may be overlooked. The law says that an option holder can use previously acquired shares in his company as payment in the exercise of a later stock option. This could be a hidden treasure. An illustration:

Betty Jones, an MBA from Harvard, joins the XYZ Corporation in Silicon Valley in northern California. Betty is a specialist in computer management and planning and is compensated at a salary of $40,000. At the time of her hiring, she agrees that she will buy 5,000 shares in XYZ at $1 per share, which she does. She also receives a stock option for 25,000 shares at $1 per share. Betty waits three years, and with the stock of XYZ up to $5 per share, she exercises her option, paying with the 5,000 shares she already holds.

Betty now has 25,000 shares worth—at the current price— $125,000. And she has parted with only $5,000 in cash to get them. Moreover, she can carry out this purchase as a tax-free transaction. She owes the IRS no tax at all—until the day she sells the shares. What is more, if Betty holds the shares for over one year, she will be taxed at the low capital gains tax rate. There is no better advantage found anywhere in the tax law.

Restrictions on ISOs

Yet the rules never cease, it seems. There are still more restrictions attached to the new incentive stock options:

• The options must be exercised only by the executive or his heirs. This means that you can't assign your spouse the right to exercise a new ISO during your lifetime, even in a divorce settlement. This becomes a touchy point of negotiation in a separation or divorce agreement. Here the lawyers must hit upon a formula to compensate for the fact that the executive may have a considerable part of his or her wealth tied up in stock options. Also, the rule means that you can't sell your right to exercise an option or pledge it for a loan at a bank. You can exercise the option, then pledge the shares, if you wish.

• The option may not be granted to an over-10-percent shareholder of the corporation unless it is granted at an option price of at least 110 percent of the fair market value (at the time the option is granted) and the option, by its terms, is not exercisable more than five years from the date of the grant. Normally, an ISO will be granted at 100 percent of the then fair market value of the stock—usually the market price in a listed company, or the reasonably determined price if it is a closed corporation not listed on a stock exchange and traded only among a small, private group. The ISO option price may not be under the current price or value, so that an executive getting an ISO must start fresh in terms of the prosperity of the company and his own option reward in the future. You can't get a leg-up by getting an option at a bargain price below market. If it is a closely held company, as in a family corporation, the option price must be 110 percent of current value, assuming the person picking up the option owns 10 percent or more of the outstanding shares of the firm. Be aware of this if you are considering joining a family corporation or if you are an owner of one.

• In any calendar year, only options to buy up to $100,000 in stock (measured by the price at the date of the grant of the option) per individual will be treated as an ISO. Thus, there is a limit that rules out the ISO as a device for luring and holding top management executives of the largest companies who might demand $1 million options. But even these people can be served by the ISO by the company granting options on a yearly installment basis: $100,000 per year per executive, year after year. Additionally, if the option granted in one year is less than the $100,000 limit, then 50 percent of the unused limit can be carried over for three years to be added to future $100,000 limits. Indeed, this new tax law doesn't miss an angle.

• ISOs must be exercised in the order in which they are granted. This rule may be described as a sleeper. A company cannot grant one option at $20, wait a year and grant another at $15 when the stock is down in price, and then permit the executive to exercise the second option first. This move was tried with the qualified option in past years, and too much juggling of options caused trouble with the IRS.

Time Restrictions Under the New Law

The new incentive options are dovetailed with earlier options. Thus, the tax law applies generally to the limited number of qualified options granted after 1975—under earlier qualified option plans. However, for options granted since 1975, there is a limit of $50,000 per year, determined at the time of the grant. Moreover, a total of only $200,000 can now qualify for ISO treatment. Any outstanding options in excess of these limits will be treated as taxable, nonqualified stock options.

Finally, employers are given one year from enactment of the new legislation (until August 13, 1982) to modify options granted on or after January 1, 1976, so that they conform to the new ISO rules. Such a modification does not require adjusting the option price to bring it in line with current stock values—a considerable advantage for many optionees.

One point regarding the question of when the Treasury (via the IRS) will issue timely regulations to clarify parts of this law: The truth is, the Treasury is slow—it has some 300 regulations (at this writing) that remain unissued, dating to new tax laws as far back as the 1976 tax reform act. They have at least 50 additional regulations to tackle because of the 1981 tax law—so don't hold your breath waiting for safe and sound rules on various fine points regarding options (which comprise an especially arcane section of the new law).

An illustration may clear up some points. Consider the case of Betty Jones. Betty receives an ISO to buy 1,000 shares of XYZ Corporation at today's price of $10 a share. Of course she works for XYZ and will do so at least until three months before she exercises her option. She waits and exercises the option when the stock sells for $20. She holds the shares for another year and then sells at the same price—$20. Leaving out a few details—such as how Betty Jones finances the 1,000 shares—here is a comparison between how she would fare first, with a nonqualified stock option, which is treated similarly to salary compensation, and secondly, with an ISO:

The nonqualified option result:
- Jones's personal profit (compensation) $10,000
- Tax due at exercise of option, assuming Jones to be in the top 50 percent marginal tax bracket. $5,000
- Tax due in the year of the sale   0
- Net benefit to Jones. $5,000

The ISO result:
- Jones's personal profit. $10,000
- Tax at time of exercise   0
- Tax in the year of sale at 20 percent capital gains rate $2,000
- Net benefit to Jones $8,000

Not sensational, you say? No, but the above numbers illustrate an average application of an ISO. But suppose Jones got the option at $10 and five years later exercised it at $30, $40 or $50. Such a stock option can really boost net worth. True, the ISO is expensive for the company—the firm loses the benefit of taking a tax deduction for the option price spread at the time of exercise, whereas using a nonqualified option permits this tax advantage. In fact, in the above example, the company actually pays $4,600 more in taxes with an ISO than with a nonqualified option on its books—to give you, the executive, an additional benefit of $3,000 on your option price. So when you ask for an ISO, push the point that you want to ride up with the fortunes of the business, but do this knowing that the company will have to bear an added expense in taxes owed the government. It won't show on the company books as expense, but it will show on the corporate tax return.

Rules Regarding "Perks"

Apart from stock options, executives are helped under the new law by a directive to the Treasury Department not to issue new regulations on the tax treatment of certain executives' perquisites, or "perks." The story is this: The IRS in the past, in the Carter White House years, made an effort to clamp down on some special rewards that executives enjoy, starting with President Carter's war on the "three-martini lunch"—as if three martinis were the usual routine at tax-deductible business lunches. In any case, in the process of attacking the "3-M" lunch, the Carter Treasury Department aimed some restrictions at other "perks"—mainly, anything in lieu of cash paid by a company to an employee.

This list included free rides in airliners for airline employees, free hotel rooms for hotel employees, cut-rate prices on merchandise for those who work for retailers, and free tuition for the sons and daughters of college professors. However, the list also includes rides in company-owned jets for personal purposes and the use of company-paid apartments such as those maintained in big cities for executives on the job—but used for personal purposes by many. Hunting lodges owned and maintained by a company for entertaining customers when used personally by executives, company cars, and company-paid limousine services used for purely personal purposes—all were on the Treasury list.

Then Congress decided to throw a net over a gung ho Treasury Department, which wanted executives and others to pay income taxes on the value of such benefits. A tempest over petty matters, in a way, and yet these perks are an item of personal importance to many executives. The upshot was that Congress specifically instructed the Treasury not to take action in this area until June 1, 1981. When that deadline passed, it was apparent that very few people in Washington or any place else really wanted to abolish the perks, so once again Congress issued instructions. It again prohibited the Treasury from issuing regulations on the taxation of such fringe benefits, and this prohibition—in the new tax law—is extended until December 31, 1983.

Tax Shelters

Tax shelter investments are treated in different ways in the new law. The picture, as a review of the law will show, is mixed. First, a look at the down side:

Elimination of the highest tax rates—those above the 50 percent marginal bracket—fairly well crimps many tax shelter investments. If your top marginal bracket is 50 percent, you can often rely pretty much on normal tax deductions and exemptions and do without the relief provided by tax sheltering via investments that always have been designed mostly for people in brackets between 50 percent and 70 percent. At 50 percent, other investments may be better for you.

The nub of it is this: When you buy a tax shelter investment, what you do, in effect, is buy a large tax deduction that can be used to offset part of your other taxable income. You invest in an oil field, for example, and as a limited partner in the venture, deduct as business expense as much as 75 percent to 100 percent of your initial investment (see below). If your tax bracket is 70 percent, each dollar's worth of deduction saves you 70 cents—and that is not bad. However, a 50 percent bracket taxpayer does not fare as well. You purchase your big deduction via the tax shelter, but each dollar of deduction saves you only 50 cents.

In analyzing many tax-sheltered investments, taxpayers in the highest bracket have been accustomed to computing an after-tax rate of return on a investment, which assumes a maximum tax rate of 60 to 70 percent. Often this has been the deciding factor in making an investment. But under the new law—for tax years beginning after December 31, 1981—the maximum of 50 percent takes the luster off many tax shelter deals. Any deduction arising from a tax-sheltered investment will offset other income at a maximum rate of just 50 percent. This will materially alter the rate-of-return analysis for many taxpayers.

Let's use Marian Evans as an example. Suppose she is pondering a possible investment in a tax shelter because she is in the 70 percent tax bracket (or was) and wants to beat the IRS. If she invests, say, $1,000, she finds that she can deduct 80 percent of it in the first year—a good deal in many tax shelters. Here's the difference between her position as a 70 percent taxpayer, and what it would be if she were a 50 percent taxpayer under the new law:

• Old law in 1981: Evans puts in $1,000. She has a tax deduction of $800—and a tax savings of 70 percent times $800, or $560.

• New law beginning in tax year 1982: Evans puts the same $1,000 in, gets the same $800 deduction, picks up a tax saving of 50 percent times $800, or $400. The bloom is off the sophisticated tax shelter investment. At least, it is on this basis.

The difference in tax savings is $560 versus $400, or $160

for each $1,000 Marian Evans invests. If you have been in a tax bracket over 50 percent, ponder this and pick up some specific advice before going into any type of tax shelter investment in 1982. Don't be suckered into a tax shelter for the sake of taxes alone. Go into one only if the basic economics of the investment appear to be sound. Tax shelters, henceforth, will succeed more on their investment quality—as a business venture—and not so much on tax gimmickry.

The Commodity Straddle

One type of tax shelter—the commodity tax straddle—has been so subject to abuse that the authors of the new tax law agreed to eliminate it. The straddle—which is based on a manipulation of two or more commodity futures contracts—enabled a high-income taxpayer to pick up big tax losses in the current year and, of course, use these losses to offset other taxable income. At the same time, the taxpayer would have gains on the transaction but with these postponed to the following year. Thus, a taxpayer could have a usable tax loss in 1982 and a *profit* from the same investment the next year. The new tax law quashes this maneuver, and if you are one of the several thousand taxpayers who "straddled" to save taxes, you'll have to seek another type of shelter.

Beware

Two important points about tax shelters:

First, you will—if you are smart—be cynical about any tax shelter deal that presents what appears at first glance to be a pipe dream. Too many tax shelter originators, promoters, and retail sellers are playing it too loose with the facts that they present to buyers, including such customers as high-income executives and professionals who should know better. Even the big brokerage houses sell shelter deals that offer little real advantage to the buyer.

Second, the IRS has had for years a war going to stamp out phony shelter deals—deals that step outside the law. This was true under the Carter Administration and is equally true under the present Reagan Administration. Don't make the mistake of assuming that because the Reaganites are sympathetic with business they also are willing to close an eye to questionable tax dodges. They are not, and the Reagan-appointed commissioner of the Internal Revenue Service, Roscoe Egger, a former Price Waterhouse executive, is as anti-tax-dodge as any previous IRS commissioner.

The phoniness in professionally sold tax shelter investments takes several forms. For example, the prospectus is often long, tedious, and obviously not intended to be read or understood by laymen. Buried in the numbers are fees and commissions for the organizers and promoters which are far out of line in view of the economics of the particular shelter. Moreover, the cash flow—the yearly return you can expect to get—is somehow so buried in the numbers as to be almost impossible for anybody but a CPA to calculate or understand. The lesson: Be cautious—especially because the new 1981 tax law does little to curb flimsy shelter investments offered to the public.

Chapter 8

Playing the Capital Gains Game

In the language of the Internal Revenue Service, there are two types of taxable gains—"long-term" and "short-term." Long-term capital gains are investments paying off or maturing after one year and one day after they were purchased. Examples of long-term capital gains:

- Shares of stocks sold two years after they were purchased.
- A parcel of land held for six years and then placed on the market.
- A 36-month bank certificate paying out at the time of maturity.
- A classic automobile sold eight years after it was bought.
- Antiques collected, then auctioned after eighteen months in storage in the attic.

In each of these examples, the investment was held longer than a year and a day.

Examples of short-term gains:

- Limited-edition prints sold four months after they were purchased.
- A $1,000 bond maturing in 30 days.
- Shares of a small business bought and liquidated within one year.

• A strip of land held for six months, then sold to the state for use in construction of a new highway.

From these illustrations, it is obvious that the way gains are taxed has little to do with the types of investments an individual makes. Rather, the tax is based on the time the investments ultimately take to pay off: Those producing long-term capital gains are taxed at a lower rate: the capital gains rate.

Understanding Capital Gains Taxation

Long-term Capital Gains. Contrary to popular assumptions, the tax levied on long-term capital gains is *not* a set rate. Rather, it is determined first by a percentage set by the federal government, then by the marginal tax bracket of the taxpayer. For example, the new and former tax laws say that individuals pay taxes on only 40 percent of the profit made on long-term capital gains investments. (The new tax law does *not* change this 60 percent deduction—leaving 40 percent of your profit taxable.) The laws also say that the tax to be paid is computed by multiplying a person's marginal tax rate by 40 percent of the amount of the gain.

A taxpayer in the 49 percent marginal tax bracket, for example, sells a parcel of land for a long-term capital gain of $50,000. He will pay taxes on 40 percent of the $50,000—or a total of $20,000. His tax bill on the $20,000 will be $9,800, which is $20,000 times 49 percent.

Another example: Let us pretend that your top tax bracket is 37 percent (e.g., a married individual filing a joint return with a taxable income of $35,000). This means you will pay an effective tax rate on long-term capital gains of 14.8 percent (37 percent tax rate times 40 percent of capital gains).

The key point here is that the tax bite on capital gains is not nearly as severe as you may think.

THE CAPITAL GAINS GAME

• You are married, file a joint return, and are in a 49 percent marginal bracket, meaning that your income ranges between $60,000 and $85,000. Any long-term capital gains you earn are taxed at a rate of 19.6 percent.

• You are in the same $60,000 income range and file a single person's return. Your top marginal bracket is 50 percent, and your capital gains rate is 20 percent.

• You are in a 33 percent bracket (income in the $30,000 range) and file a joint return. Your capital gains rate is 13.2 percent.

• Or you are in the same $30,000 income range and single and your tax bracket is 40 percent. Your capital gains rate is 16 percent—still not bad!

To determine your capital gains tax rate, use this two-step formula: First, multiply 40 percent by the profit on your investment. Then multiply the result of that first step by your tax bracket. (A selection of marginal tax rates is provided in figure 2–2. You may want to refer to it.) The resulting percentage is your capital gains rate.

Short-Term Capital Gains. No short-term capital gains tax advantage is provided by the federal government. On the contrary, profits on these investments are treated in the same manner as personal income and are taxed at the same rate. For instance, if you are in a 46 percent tax bracket, 46 percent of your short-term capital gains go to the Internal Revenue Service. The same is true no matter what your tax bracket or how much you earn from your investments.

How Capital Gains
Have Been Changed

The new tax law *does* change the way short-term and long-term gains are taxed, but it *does not* specifically order a reduction in the capital gains tax rate. Instead, it lowers the capital gains rate indirectly by reducing all marginal tax rates and especially by reducing the maximum tax rate on an individual's income from 70 percent to 50 percent—no matter how high the income. Formerly, earned income—meaning salaries and bonuses—was taxed at a maximum rate of 50 percent, while unearned income—primarily from dividends, interest on investments and so on—was taxed up to 70 percent. Under the Reagan tax law, 50 percent is the overall maximum. The effect is to reduce the long-term capital gains tax rate from a maximum of 28 percent to 20 percent and to place a 50 percent ceiling on short-term capital gains taxation.

To illustrate, two examples:

• James Hines is married and for the year 1980 filed a joint income tax return. On it he listed $60,000 in profits from capital gains investments. On that amount, he paid a tax of $16,320—a figure computed in the following manner: 40 percent times $60,000 equals $24,000; $24,000 times 68 percent—Hines's 1980 tax rate—equals $16,320. (That translates into a capital gains tax rate of 27.2 percent.) For the tax year 1982, Hines files an identical return, listing the same amount of earnings from long-term investments. He records a capital gains tax liability of $12,000—a figure that is $4,320 less than—and a full 7 percentage points below—his 1980 tax level. Hines's tax burden has dipped because, under the Reagan plan, his marginal tax rate has dropped from 68 percent to 50 percent (40 percent times $60,000 equals $24,000; $24,000 times 50 percent—Hines's 1984 tax rate—equals $12,000).

• Benjamin and Barbara Green are young physicians. They move in September of 1984 to rural Wyoming and tack an "open for business" sign on the side of the house they purchase for $50,000—with the help of the local bank. In December of 1984, a patient offers to buy the house from them for $60,000—a $10,000 profit. The couple discuss the matter, then decide to sell. Listed on the tax return they file on April 15, 1985, is a short-term capital gain of $10,000. This is added to their otherwise low income: The Greens—their practice still young—in 1984 will jointly amass taxable earnings of $25,000, which alone will place them in a 25 percent tax bracket. The $10,000 short-term gain on the sale of the house will push them into another tax bracket, and their marginal rate will rise to 28 percent. They multiply 28 percent by $35,000 and arrive at the figure $9,800—their total federal tax liability for that year. (They keep $7,200 of their $10,000 profit on the sale of the house.)

Alternative Minimum Tax

Some American taxpayers—a small percentage—receive the majority of their income from investments. These individuals have exceptionally high long-term capital gains and often high amounts of itemized deductions (interest, charitable contributions, investment expenses, etc.). As a rule, they owe the government a supplementary tax called the "alternative minimum tax." (The proper name of this tax is Alternative Minimum Taxable Income and it is often referred to as AMTI.)

The idea behind the alternative minimum tax is that these taxpayers, because of the unique makeup of their income and offsetting deductions, might otherwise escape an equitable amount of taxation.

The formula used to compute this tax is arcane: Usually three items are added together:

• First, your taxable income for the year.

• Second, the 60 percent, nontaxable part of your capital gains income for the year.

• And finally an adjusted amount covering any unusual, extremely high tax deductions.

Of this total, the first $20,000 is exempted from the special tax. The next $40,000 is taxed at 10 percent. The following $40,000 is taxed at 20 percent, and, finally, the remainder—any amount over $100,000—is taxed at 25 percent.

In a typical case where the taxable income is $60,000, and

the two other elements add up to $90,000, the resulting AMTI is $150,000. Applying the formula, the special tax comes to about $25,000. The regularly computed tax—in this case it is $20,000—is subtracted, for a net AMTI tax of $5,000.

The new law makes a seemingly small change, but it will be important to people with exceptionally high amounts of capital gains from investments. The Economic Recovery Tax Act conforms the alternative minimum tax to the maximum capital gains tax by reducing the top alternative minimum tax rate from 25 percent to 20 percent effective for taxable years beginning after 1981. A special rule is provided for 1981 to ensure that capital gains on sales or exchanges after June 9, 1981, will not be subject to an alternative minimum tax rate greater than 20 percent.

Under the new rule, the first $20,000 is still exempted. The rate for the next $40,000 is still 10 percent, and the rate for any greater amount is 20 percent. If you are in this position—having to apply the AMTI formula—you will want the fine print of your tax return for 1981 to be puzzled through by an expert, preferably a certified public accountant or a tax attorney.

Survival Strategies

Taking advantage of the resulting reduction in capital gains tax rates is reasonably simply—if you know the schedule for implementing the tax cuts (see chapter 2). The key items to remember:

• The 20 percent maximum tax on long-term capital gains is retroactive to June 9, 1981. The intention here was to prevent taxpayers in the higher tax brackets—50 percent to 70 percent—from postponing taking capital gains profits until later years.

• A 50 percent cap on short-term capital gains taxation is effective beginning January 1, 1982. This means that the maximum tax on profits from investments—"unearned income"—

is equal to the top tax rate on salaries, wages and bonuses paid to us for our services. (Pensions also are considered as earned income.) Previously, short-term investment income could be taxed at a rate as high as 70 percent—a situation that added to the popularity of tax shelters. Congress debated this issue hotly—the Democrats wanted to phase the reduction in over two years—a 60 percent ceiling in 1982, a 50 percent cap in 1983. Eventually, the decision was made to make the single cut in January of 1982.

• For taxpayers who are not in the higher brackets, the long-term and short-term capital gains cuts come with reductions in the withholding taxes—1.25 percent in 1981, 10 percent in 1982 and 10 percent in 1983.

In attempting to determine how you can make use of the tax cuts, you should first consider your tax bracket, then plot your timing to coincide with the cuts:

• *High-Income Taxpayers.* If you are a high-income taxpayer, there is no tax advantage in rearranging the times when you will receive earnings from long-term investments. Postponing these earnings from one year to another will not help. The retroactive rule—effectively reducing the long-term capital gains rate to a top of 20 percent last year—contained in the Economic Recovery Tax Act provides you with a big break now. Make use of it, but have a tax advisor check your paperwork on sales of long-term investments before you file your 1981 income tax return.

An example: David Jones is single and is a 70 percent bracket taxpayer in 1981. His taxable income in 1981 is $110,000—above the $107,700 line that put him into the 70 percent marginal bracket. He netted $50,000 in long-term capital gains profits early in 1981 from the sale of investment property. His tax on his gain—payable on April 15, 1982—comes to 40 percent times 70 percent times $50,000, or $14,000, which is a tax of 28 percent. In 1983, Jones, again filing a single person's return, will list a long-term capital gain of $50,000 for 1982. In

1983 he will pay a tax of $10,000, or 20 percent (40 percent times 50 percent times $50,000). His tax for 1982 on his capital gain will be $4,000 less than in 1981—a drop in tax amounting to 28.6 percent. That's not bad.

• *Low- and Middle-Income Taxpayers*. The retroactive clause in the new tax law is of no help to low- or middle-income taxpayers. That is why you should consider delaying profits on long-term and short-term investments until the tax rates decrease. Postponing earnings from late 1981 into early 1982, from late 1982 into early 1983 or from late 1983 into early 1984, should cause you little pain and will enable you to keep more of what you make.

For all types of taxpayers, it is even possible to nail down a 1982 paper profit and have it taxed in 1983, when the rates used by the IRS will be lower. In effect, you freeze a profit (or loss) and postpone the tax result by using a "short sale." For example, to fix the current paper profit in a block of stock, you go to your stockbroker and tell him you want to arrange a short sale. He'll set it up for you. It will work something like this:

• You own 100 shares of the XYZ Corporation. The stockbroker allows you to borrow another 100, using your existing shares as collateral.

• You then sell the borrowed shares, thus fixing your profit.

• In January of next year, you don't owe the stockbroker money; you owe him shares. You deliver your original shares to the broker in repayment.

The result: The capital gain (profit) on the 1982 short sale becomes next year's taxable income. The maneuver can work beautifully purely as a tax move—but its viability depends more on the price movement of the block of stock. Obviously, a short sale to pick up a 10 percent tax advantage means little if the stock turns up far beyond current expectations.

Chapter 9

How U.S. Expatriates Can Get Rich

The Economic Recovery Tax Act provides a huge tax break to U.S. expatriate workers *and* their employers—in fact, up to $75,000 of salary or wages can be excluded from an employee's U.S. taxable income, in 1982. This steps up to $95,000 in 1986. So great is the enthusiasm for this break that already a steadily increasing number of Americans are seeking—and being offered—lucrative jobs abroad. Yet there is more to this new section of the tax law than meets the eye, and to understand what the law really does, it is necessary to know some of the background.

The new law, in fact, answers a plea that was voiced in two years of dogged lobbying by certain industries having far-flung operations overseas. The construction, oil, airline, and some manufacturing industries wanted a large chunk of personal income earned by Americans overseas *excluded* from taxation in the United States. They needed this, they said, because the U.S. was the only industrial nation that taxed the earnings of its citizens working in other countries. Americans, in essence (meaning the companies), were being placed at a competitive disadvantage. The tax system by which U.S. expatriates working abroad were taxed *twice*—by the U.S. and by the resident country—was creating economic hardship for

American corporations, which often found it hard to compete with foreign companies because the U.S. employers—because of the tax system—were faced with much higher labor costs.

Moreover, said the lobbyists in Washington, the tax relief was needed—a new law, that is—to replace the unworkable and unfairly costly tax law that had been in place since 1978. That law—the Foreign Earned Income Tax Act—involved a complex series of tax deductions covering workers' housing, their children's education, and an array of other expenses. In turn, it supplanted much simpler legislation that had allowed Americans working outside the country to exclude the first $25,000 of income from U.S. taxation. The $25,000 was outdated, so the lobbyists maintained, but the idea—an exclusion—was the needed remedy.

Indeed, the 1978 law was too complex (to the point of being arcane), and it led to extremely high taxation. In fact, in 1981 the international accountants Ernst & Whinney, in a major study, managed to prove the point over and over. For example, they estimated that a U.S. company employing a worker who was married, had one child, earned $40,000 a year, and worked in Saudi Arabia, would save $7,200 a year if U.S. taxes were eliminated. In Kuwait, the saving to the company would be $9,500, and in Oman, nearly $12,000. Note two points: First that *countries* are given in the example (which tells something about the new law, to be explained in a moment); and, too, that the companies, not the workers, would save on taxes.

The fact was that starting in 1979, many U.S. multinational companies began coping with the high taxes by sending fewer Americans to work abroad. A 1981 estimate by the General Accounting Office in Washington, D.C., showed the U.S. expatriate work-force to be 20 percent smaller than it would have been had the tax on expatriates' income not gone up in 1978. There also was ample speculation that the tax had the effect of cutting into U.S. exports and, thus, into U.S.

Treasury revenues. Such claims dotted a number of industry-sponsored reports, undertaken mainly by the construction and oil industries and others having large numbers of employees in the Middle East, where the greatest tax disadvantages were felt.

These arguments were difficult to verify, but they were persuasive enough to impress Congress and Reagan Administration officials. The end result: the Economic Recovery Tax Act's new rules for taxing American expatriates. Industry got what it wanted, and business began predicting that more Americans would be sent abroad to work in future years and more high-income jobs would be created.

Still, if you are an American employed abroad—or considering a job abroad—don't start counting up your tax savings. True, accountants estimate that the new law will lower the net tax bills for those who work in foreign countries by about 25 percent. Yet the benefits provided under the new law probably will be gained, not by you personally, but by your employer. The reason is that most major corporations have what are called tax equalization policies. The idea of these is that workers' wages and salaries are adjusted so that their take-home pay equals what it would have been were they stationed in the U.S. Thus, by lowering the taxes of American expatriate employees, the government has helped the multinational companies in most cases, not the individuals.

This leads to the second elusive point: the varied impact of the new tax law from country to country. The uneven effect exists because under both past law and the new law, the amount an expatriate pays to the U.S. Treasury is based primarily on the difference between the foreign taxes and U.S. taxes owed. That is, U.S. taxes are subject to an offset.

If the foreign income tax is *greater* than the tax owed to the U.S. Treasury, then no tax is paid in the U.S. The full foreign tax is paid, of course, with no American tax due.

Lowering the U.S. tax, in such a case, does not help the American expatriate. Thus, in a country where the tax rate is higher than in the U.S., there is no help in the new law for either U.S. companies or their employees. The result is that the new tax law will bring *no* net savings from expatriate employment in most countries in Western Europe or Latin America or Japan, since most have higher tax rates than the U.S. maximum rate of 50 percent.

If the foreign taxes are *lower* than taxes in the U.S., as in the Middle East and a few other areas, the Economic Recovery Tax Act will have a saving effect. The new law says that no longer will a U.S. tax be due on the difference between the lower foreign tax rate and the U.S. rate—up to the fixed amount of earnings the new law permits U.S. workers to exclude from taxable income: that is, $75,000 for the 1982 tax year. Thus, U.S. workers in the Middle East, or their employers, will gain a substantial tax advantage. In fact, the primary beneficiaries will be the multinational construction and oil companies because they operate widely in the Middle East, where there are virtually no income taxes.

Some U.S. multinationals, especially in construction, will have direct savings of at least $10 million in 1982, and far more in later years. In turn, it is hoped that they will be more competitive in bidding against foreign companies for contracts, and this may produce more jobs for Americans abroad.

There will be great tax savings in store for *individual Americans* who either work abroad in the Middle East or other low-tax areas for companies that make no attempt to "equalize" net earnings (that is, earnings after taxes) or work as self-employed individuals or in small, closely owned companies in which they are part owners. You—as an individual—could go abroad to a low-tax country, get a job for a local company there, or work as a self-employed person, and gain the full benefit of the $75,000 tax exclusion for 1982.

Figure 9–1 shows the countries in which U.S. expatriates

and U.S. corporations will save tax money under the new tax law.

FIGURE 9–1

WHERE AMERICANS CAN AND CANNOT SAVE ON TAXES

Countries	Maximum Tax Rate (%) Applied to U.S. Nationals
Where Employment Produces the Biggest Savings:	
Bahamas	0
Bahrain	0
Britain	30*
Hong Kong	15
Kuwait	0
Oman	0
Saudi Arabia	5
Venezuela	45

* Effective maximum tax rate for foreign nationals.

Where Savings Are Not Available:	
Belgium	67
Brazil	55
Canada	60†
France	60
Italy	72
Japan	75
Mexico	55
Singapore	55
West Germany	56

† Composite tax rate: federal and provincial rates.

SOURCE: ERNST & WHINNEY INTERNATIONAL

How the New Law Works

In the Bahamas, for example, a U.S. expatriate could thrive. Since there is no income tax there, the full benefit of the

1982 exclusion of $75,000 would apply. No wonder there has been a rush to jobs in *some* countries abroad. The same holds true in the Mideast oil countries, of course, while in Britain an American could save the difference between the British 30 percent tax rate and his or her U.S. bracket—assuming that he or she would be subject to a higher tax rate in the U.S. The pickings are lean, however, on the Continent in Europe. A job in West Germany or France, for instance, would cost more in taxes than a job in the U.S. if the American was not protected by a corporate tax equalization plan.

In any case, the Economic Recovery Tax Act provides an entirely new set of rules—reasonably simple rules—governing the way you will be taxed if and when you decide to work abroad. The law's principal provision establishes a fixed level of earnings which U.S. expatriate workers may exclude from taxation by the United States. You will, of course, always be subject to taxation based on your income earned in the country in which you live and work if that country imposes income taxes.

The new rules provide that if Americans meet certain residency requirements, (discussed in a moment) they may exclude $75,000 of their earned income in 1982, with this amount increasing in $5,000 jumps until 1986, when $95,000 will be excluded from U.S. taxation (see figure 9–2). Industry estimates are that 90 percent or more of all Americans working abroad will be covered by the initial $75,000 exclusion—good news for expatriates and employers alike. For the 10 percent or fewer expatriates whose annual earnings are *greater* than the U.S. exclusion for the year, the excess amount is combined with other taxable income and is taxed accordingly by the U.S.

Note that the $75,000 (up to $95,000) exclusion encompasses only "foreign earned income." This is defined specifically, and it covers wages, salaries, bonuses, and other direct earnings paid to Americans living and working abroad. It does *not* cover income from a pension or annuity, or wages

Figure 9-2

EXCLUSION SCHEDULE FOR
FOREIGN EARNED INCOME

For Taxable Years Beginning in:	Annual Exclusion:
1982	$75,000
1983	80,000
1984	85,000
1985	90,000
1986 and later years	95,000

paid by the U.S. government to federal employees, or amounts contributed by an employer to an employee's pension program. Income from these sources is treated as U.S.-earned income and is taxed accordingly.

Those who earn *more* than the fixed excludable amount for the year get an added advantage—a little-known plum in the new law. The taxable part of their income is, of course, subject to the current marginal tax brackets—but the rates begin at the *bottom of the tax tables*. For instance, if your taxable foreign earned income is $85,000 in 1982, which is $10,000 above the exclusion, the additional $10,000 will be taxed at the same rate paid by a U.S. taxpayer whose total taxable income for the year is $10,000. For a single taxpayer, this rate is 19 percent in 1982, and for a married person filing a joint return, it is 16 percent—a far cry from the 49 percent marginal rate that applies to those whose taxable income—in the U.S.—is $85,000.

This plum extends to investment income, and for most taxpayers this is another hidden boon in the new law. The rule is that an individual's investment income: dividends, interest, rents, royalties etc.—is to be taxed as if it were "the first income earned." Meaning, of course, taxed in the marginal brackets starting at the bottom. For example, a $75,000 (taxable) executive living and working abroad, who has $10,000 of investment income from U.S. sources, with a taxable total of $85,000, would in 1982 pay *no* U.S. tax on the earned $75,000—and, again, either 16 or 19 percent on the $10,000.

New Rules on Foreign Housing

Another new benefit is a separate exclusion, *or* a tax deduction, to help compensate for high foreign housing costs—currently those in excess of some $6,000 a year. Which you qualify for depends on the terms of your employment:

• If your company provides you with housing (such as a rent-free apartment, or pays a cash housing allowance, then probably you are eligible for the tax exclusion. This means that you do not report the allowance or value of the housing as taxable income. Instead, the exclusion is figured this way: All housing costs (rent, insurance, utilities, maintenance, etc.) are valued and totaled. From this amount, you subtract $6,059 (an amount based on the similar allowance of a Grade-14 federal employee). The remainder—the amount in excess of $6,059—may be excluded from your taxable earnings *in addition* to the basic earned income exclusion (maximum $75,000 in 1982).

For example, if a taxpayer's salary is $75,000 and the value of housing provided by the employer is $27,500, the total U.S. tax exclusion is $75,000 plus [$27,500 − $6,059], or $96,441. In a similar case, the exclusion in 1986, with the earned income exclusion up to $95,000, would be a healthy *$116,441*. Indeed, the Washington lobbyists managed quite a coup.

• If your company *does not* provide housing or a housing allowance, then probably you qualify for a tax deduction in lieu of the added exclusion. The deduction equals the excess of your actual housing costs (rent, insurance, utilities, etc.) over the currently allowed base amount of $6,059. If your housing costs were $27,500 for the year, the deduction would be

$27,500 minus $6,059, or $21,441—which, if added to an earned income exclusion of $75,000, would come to $96,441.

Two important points to keep in mind are that—

• Deciding whether you qualify for a housing exclusion or a tax deduction is not as simple as it appears to be. The law is somewhat unclear in its definition of what constitutes "employer-provided" housing or a housing "allowance." Checking with an accountant or the employer, or the IRS, may be wise, although a Treasury ruling may have clarified the point in the meantime.

• The amount of money you spend maintaining a home in the U.S. (over and above any rental income) is *not* tax deductible, nor may you use it in determining your housing costs abroad.

Living in "camps" abroad—traditionally some form of spartan housing in a remote locale, provided by an employer—has been made less unpleasant by the new tax law. The law keeps the basic rule that when a worker is furnished housing in a foreign camp location, the housing—for tax purposes—is treated as part of the company's business premises. Thus, the value of meals and lodging is not counted as taxable income to the employee, under well-established general tax rules. The new law adds two liberalizations:

• A camp—in a reversal of past law—need *not* be located in a "hardship" area: meaning in the wilds; nor need it be classified as "substandard" housing to be nontaxable to the employee. This means that a company hostel, or apartments, or row houses, for example, might be located in a hamlet in England or France, near a plant development—and might be of high standard in terms of living quality—and still be nontaxable to the employees required to live there as part of their employment agreement.

• The individual expatriate can exclude the value of such a camp—furnished by the company—even though he or she does not qualify for the general earned income exclusion or the additional housing exclusion or deduction. An employee might not qualify, for example, because of failing to fulfill foreign residency requirements (see below).

Moving expenses of expatriate workers are subject to no new rules, possibly since the old rules are quite liberal. If your company reimburses or pays directly for your foreign moving expenses, the amount should be reported as part of your earned income. However, if a taxpayer begins work at a foreign location, there is a reasonable tax deduction possible for house-hunting trips and temporary living costs incurred while a new home is sought. The top limit on this is $4,500. These expenses plus additional expenses for home sale, home purchase, or lease making, may be deducted up to $6,000. The time-period for avoiding taxable gain on a home sale and replacement—that is, a tax-free rollover—is four years, in a transaction involving U.S.–foreign locations (see chapter 5).

Travel to the new location by both you and your family, and the cost of shipping household items are fully deductible. If you must store furniture and personal possessions while working out of the country, the charges may be treated as related to moving, and are deductible, year to year.

Qualifying Under the Expatriate Rules

Before you jump to conclusions about garnering the valuable tax advantages of working abroad, it will be wise to make sure that you qualify. Under the new law, American expatriates must meet one of two tests to be eligible for the tax breaks provided. These are the bona fide residence test and the physical presence test.

• *Bona Fide Residence*. Qualifying under this test means that you must have lived for an *uninterrupted* period of time— a minimum of one year—in the foreign country. Uninterrupted means that you are not allowed to travel outside the country. Once you have qualified under this test, the law allows you to amend already-filed tax returns to reflect your foreign residency status. A point to keep in mind is that this is not the same as mere domicile. Bona fide residence is determined by the length of your stay and by the *nature* of your stay. You must work full-time and live full-time in a foreign country to pass this test.

• *Physical Presence*. Under this test, an American expatriate must spend a minimum of 330 days in a 12-month period in the foreign country. The definition of a day is the normal 24-hour period. The 12 months must be consecutive.

These tests sound similar, but there are important differences. Here is an example:

John Grant, his wife, Faye, and their two children move to a foreign country on June 15, 1982. They hold "resident visas" permitting them a three-year assignment there. However, they travel frequently to the United States, visiting friends and family, so their stay in the foreign country is "interrupted," although they maintain a home there until the end of 1983. Clearly they are disqualified under the bona fide residence test: they traveled outside the country. The Grants do pass the physical presence test, however. The reason is that they remain residents of the country for some 18 months—more than enough time to fulfill the 330-day requirement of that test.

The result: The Grants can file a 1983 joint tax return and amend their 1982 return, claiming the deductions and exclusions permitted expatriate workers.

If you are an American expatriate working abroad, your U.S. tax return should be filed by the usual date—April 15. However, as a resident abroad, you have a routine filing-time extention to June 15—but only at the cost of paying interest (20 percent in 1982) on any taxes due the IRS. If you owe $1,000 in taxes, and file on June 15, your interest expense would cover two months, and the charge would be about $33.

If you have been unable to qualify under the bona fide residence test or physical presence test (as above), you can obtain a filing-time extension if this will enable you to qualify. The proper form (No. 2350) can be had from the Revenue Service Center, Philadelphia, Pa. 19255. All tax returns of expatriates should be mailed to this address.

If you are employed (or will be employed) by a U.S. company in an office or other operation abroad, the company will no doubt offer some guidance and advice about handling your tax reporting. Many companies, in fact, bear the responsibility of the paperwork requirements of the IRS and the tax department of the foreign country, as well. Remember, however, that the business of filing tax returns is a *personal* responsibility—and some expatriates have been rudely awakened to this upon being called on the carpet by the Internal Revenue Service. Slipups can happen, and it is a mistake to rely heavily on the company. In any case, there is a list of points to be aware of in filing tax returns from a location abroad. Four items on this list are especially important in view of changes in the tax law:

• Withholding. You may want to adjust your U.S. withholding allowances, using Form W-4. Check details with your company payroll clerk, or, if you are in a small business, with the IRS or a tax accountant.

• Deductions. Assuming that you itemize deductions (medical, interest, state and local taxes, etc.), you may follow the standard instructions used in the U.S. However, keep in mind: sales taxes paid abroad are not deductible. Charitable donations to foreign charities are not deductible. Property taxes, though, generally are deductible.

• Retirement accounts. If you make annual contributions to an Individual Retirement Account (IRA) or Keogh plan, you may deduct these on your U.S. tax return in the usual manner.

• Other income. Generally (as explained earlier) you get a tax break in that investment income will be taxed in lower brackets. However, be aware that substantial income apart from the money you earn abroad may create tax problems: for instance, you might face a minimum tax (the tax that is an add-on to the normal taxes paid by most taxpayers and which affects a number of higher-income people). This sort of "other income" problem should be discussed with a tax accountant.

Chapter 10 _____

The Estate and Gift Tax Windfall

In the two centuries since Benjamin Franklin pressed an ink-dipped quill against parchment, nothing has been certain in this country but death and taxes—usually higher taxes. Now, we can thankfully say, many taxes—including those levied against the gifts we make and receive, and the estates we leave and inherit—are decreasing. Indeed, the Economic Recovery Tax Act of 1981 completely reshapes the laws on gift and estate taxation to the benefit of all who have assets. The wealthy gain much, and those of more modest means also gain. The centerpiece of the new law is that starting in 1987, up to $600,000 can be passed along to loved ones—free of taxation.

Widows, widowers, sons, daughters, all gain under the new law—particularly surviving spouses, who benefit from another rule allowing unlimited tax-free bequests to one's spouse. And the owners of family farms and family-controlled businesses (who have had special estate tax problems) come out far ahead. No longer will so many heirs of such properties be forced to sell out—simply to satisfy the appetite of the Internal Revenue Service.

Thus, the new law allows almost all of us to keep more of what we inherit and what is given to us, and the methods that make this possible are varied (they are discussed below). Yet the principal method is the "unified credit," a device created in 1976 to replace separate taxes levied on gifts and estates. The unified tax-credit has been *vastly* increased by the new 1981 law—and thus estate tax exemptions have been vastly increased, as well.

The pre-1976 estate tax law—highly obsolete—had set $60,000 as the maximum an individual could bequeath tax-free. And separate gift tax rules let you string out small gifts year to year ($3,000 per year per donee, now raised to $10,000) and allow up to $30,000 in a lump sum if you chose—all tax-free.

The unified tax credit clears the board of these separate tax rules and creates a single formula for taxation. Simply stated, the value of gifts made during your lifetime (over and above the yearly tax-free limit) is added to the total value of your estate when you die. It is your executor's job to pay federal and state taxes and make all disbursements to beneficiaries named in the will. A tax bill is computed, and if the bill is *more* than the unified tax credit—your heirs owe a tax on the excess.

The increased tax credit, in turn, translates into larger estate exemptions, and these reach higher and higher amounts as the tax credit is increased by the new law. These increases start in 1982 and continue to 1987. In the latter year, the maximum credit and estate exemption are reached. What happens is shown in figure 10–1.

This means that in 1982, up to $225,000 of estate property falls outside the scope of federal estate taxation. In 1987, the amount will go to $600,000—but be aware that $600,000 in 1987 will be far less in true dollar value than in 1982, assuming that inflation keeps eroding the dollar in double-digit amounts each year. Thus, the estates of many high-ranking employees—not just top executives—will fall into the taxable classification. This will be true, particularly through 1984, when the exempt amount will be $325,000—far below the $600,000 maximum.

Thus, many professional employees of large companies,

THE ESTATE AND GIFT TAX

Figure 10–1

	Unified Tax Credit	Estate Exempt from Taxation
Old Law		
1981	$ 47,000	$175,625
New Law		
1982	$ 62,800	$225,000
1983	79,300	275,000
1984	96,300	325,000
1985	121,800	400,000
1986	155,800	500,000
1987 and later	192,800	600,000

self-employed businessmen and businesswomen, middle management supervisors and minor executives, and successful sales people working on commissions are some of the groups who will be wise to learn more about the new estate tax law. And, of course, senior executives on high salaries would be downright foolish to ignore the new law, thinking that their estates will fall short of the taxation danger point. The new tax act gives much, but it has its limits.

What the Lower-Tax Rules Accomplish

The unified tax, which came into being in 1976—with its single unified tax credit—is carried forward strongly in the new law, and the effect is to exempt *most* estates from taxation. Remember that the credit is offset, first, by taxable lifetime gifts, presumably made to one's family. Whatever part of the credit is left over can then be used to offset taxable inherited property. To take a simplified example: In 1981 the tax credit was $47,000, and this meant that about $176,000 of otherwise taxable property could be deducted from an estate as an exemption. Thus if a widower, during his lifetime, gave $76,000 to his children, possibly in the form of a house he owned—the children could later inherit $100,000 (the remainder of the exemption) free of further taxation.

Thus, by stepping up the unified tax credit, the Economic Recovery Tax Act eliminates all gift and estate taxes for property up to $600,000 in value starting in 1987. However—and this is a point that somehow has been glossed over in the daily press—exemptions are only part of the whole story, at least, for families in the highest brackets. The tax *rates,* as well, have been lowered for taxable estates of *$2,500,000 and more.* Just as the top income tax rate has been dropped from 70 percent to 50 percent by the new law, the top rate covering large estates

FIGURE 10–2

ESTATE-GIFT TAX RATES: 1982 AND THEREAFTER

| If the taxable amount is: | | The Tax is: | | Percentage on | |
Over	But not over	Tax +		Excess over	
$ 0	$ 10,000	$ 0	+18%	$ 0	
10,000	20,000	1,800	20	10,000	
20,000	40,000	3,800	22	20,000	
40,000	60,000	8,200	24	40,000	
60,000	80,000	13,000	26	60,000	
80,000	100,000	18,200	28	80,000	
100,000	150,000	23,800	30	100,000	
150,000	250,000	38,800	32	150,000	
250,000	500,000	70,800	34	250,000	
500,000	750,000	155,800	37	500,000	
750,000	1,000,000	248,300	39	750,000	
1,000,000	1,250,000	345,800	41	1,000,000	
2,000,000	2,500,000	780,800	49	2,000,000	
2,500,000	3,000,000*	1,025,800	53	2,500,000	

* Tax on excess amount drops to 50 percent maximum in 1985.

also was dropped from 70 percent to 50 percent. The 20-point decrease is phased in from 1982 through 1985. This review concentrates on the law changes affecting families in more modest estate brackets than $2,500,000-and-up. Figure 10–2, however, shows the unified estate-gift taxes for people in all brackets. Note that the tables are computed for taxable amounts, after exemptions.

The New Marital Deduction

When it was adopted, the 1976 tax law was praised for the changes it made in the amount you were permitted to leave your spouse without estate taxes being due. That law allowed you to leave tax-free half of your estate to your husband or wife, or $250,000, whichever was greater. Thus, if your estate was worth *less* than $500,000, your spouse was exempt from the 50 percent rule. It meant that you could bequeath your entire estate valued as high as $426,000 to your spouse, and he or she could receive all of it free of taxation: $250,000 as a marital deduction, and $176,000 as an exemption. The idea was to help the great numbers of taxpayers who had been rapidly pushed by inflation into the range of estate taxes.

Another feature of the 1976 law allowed a married taxpayer to give up to $100,000 to his or her spouse during the taxpayer's lifetime free of any gift tax. It further enhanced this offer by stating that if lifetime gifts exceeded $200,000, then only 50 percent of the gifts in excess of $200,000 would be taxed.

Positive as all this sounds, the new Economic Recovery Tax Act does much better:

• First, it eliminates *all* the carefully developed but limiting provisions of 1976.

• Second, it provides an *umlimited* marital deduction to spouses inheriting estates in 1982 and later years. This is significant. You now may leave your entire estate to your spouse, and no matter how large it is, the beneficiary, being your husband or your wife, will pay no taxes on it.

Here is an illustration:

Joe Hilton is 60 years old. His wife Ruth is 40. The couple has no children. Joe, a wealthy man, dies, leaving his entire estate—$10 million—to Ruth. During his lifetime, he also had given his wife $1 million. No taxes are due. Ruth, as Joe's wife, qualifies for the marital deduction.

Here is another illustration:

Bob Woods is a corporate executive. He dies in 1987, leaving an estate valued at $750,000. He leaves half of his holdings to his wife and half to his children. No taxes are due: His widow's inheritance is not taxed; his children's inheritance falls far below the $600,000 exempt amount.

The new unlimited marital deduction does not mean that the Internal Revenue Service loses. On the contrary, it still will collect its revenue, but only after the death of the second marriage partner. In Ruth Hilton's case, the government may have to wait more than 35 years, assuming she lives out the average life expectancy.

Aside from forcing the IRS to wait, the new unlimited marital deduction may tempt many people to give or "will" larger amounts to their spouses than they would otherwise. One negative result might be that certain individuals will choose to neglect or ignore the best interests of their children in an effort to avoid estate taxes. Another possibility is that some legators, particularly those who are the principal bread-winners and who hold in their name most of the family assets, may not want to pass control of their wealth to a spouse. The spouse might be mentally or emotionally ill, might be alcoholic, or simply might not have any interest in handling the affairs of an inherited estate or business. (The answer might be the placement of such property in a trust. More about this later.)

Deciding whether to capture the full advantage of the

unlimited marital deduction is an individual issue. That is how it should be addressed, and that is how it should be decided. Generally, though—in tax terms—the question of whether to pass large amounts to a spouse under the unlimited marital deduction will depend on the result of the following formula: *The advantage of eliminating the estate tax on the property when the first spouse dies, with this tax to be paid at the time of the second spouse's death, versus the disadvantage of raising the second spouse's estate into a higher tax bracket at the time of his or her death.*

An example:

George Herd, a successful business executive, dies in 1987, leaving a widow and two children, and an estate valued at $1,500,000. According to an example posed by Arthur Andersen & Company, the national accounting firm, if Herd's will utilized the *unlimited* marital deduction, then $55,500 in estate taxes could be postponed until the death of Herd's widow, possibly many years in the future.

In past years, under the old law, the most common way to distribute such an estate would be simply a 50-50 split between the widow and the children. The 50 percent left to the surviving spouse would have been tax-free, under the earlier marital deduction rule which permitted half of an estate to be left to a spouse tax-free. The remaining 50 percent, or $750,000, willed to the children, would have been taxable. If Herd's will follows this simple device (say that he chose not to change it following the new 1981 law), the tax on the second $750,000 going to the children would be (in 1987) $248,300 (see tax table, page 133), minus the allowed tax credit of $192,800—or *$55,500.*

By a quick, easy, one-line change in his will, George Herd could have adopted the unlimited marital deduction, leaving his total estate to his spouse, free of estate taxes—*or* all but $600,000—thus postponing the payment of $55,500 for a span of years. The parallel computation for an estate of $2 million shows a postponement of *$153,000.*

What the unlimited marital deduction does, then—if you overlook its possible disadvantages and choose to use it—is postpone estate taxes during the life of the surviving spouse, usually the wife, since women outlive men by at least eight years, on average. The savings over a span of time can be substantial. For example, postponed taxes can be invested to produce income for the family: $50,000 of postponed tax money invested at 10 percent interest will earn $5,000 over a one-year period. If $5,000 is saved each year during the surviving spouse's lifetime and compounds annually at 10 percent, the result can be striking: In 10 years, the fund will swell to $79,000. Postponing $10,000 in taxes will produce even more marked results: $10,000 tucked away each year at 10 percent grows to $158,000 in a decade—a figure equal to more than 15 percent of a $1 million estate.

The "Qualified Terminable Interest"

The portion of the tax law outlining the unlimited marital deduction is supplemented by the introduction of a difficult but important concept called the "qualified terminable interest." This device makes the marital deduction more sweeping and gives an individual who writes a will considerably more power in determining the ultimate disposition of his or her property. Thus, the concept—step by step:

The underlying point to remember about a qualified terminable interest is what is called a "life estate." If you provide in your will that your spouse will have merely a life estate in a piece of property, he or she normally gets the income from the property each year and the use of the property for life only. It amounts to lifetime use and possession falling short of ownership.

Under the old law, granting a simple life estate meant that no tax would be paid on the property at the time of the surviving spouse's death. There had been no complete assignment, or gift, of ownership by the grantor to the surviving spouse, and so none could be passed on when the surviving spouse died. The result: no estate tax. Therefore, property subject to a simple life estate could not be included in the marital deduction in the estate of the spouse who had granted the life estate—the spouse who wrote the will. For the property to be considered as marital deduction property in the grantor's estate—and thus free of estate tax at the grantor's death—the surviving spouse who got the life estate also had to be given the right to name the ultimate beneficiary of the property.

The new law, in effect, reverses this rule. It allows the person writing the will to grant a life estate and name the ultimate beneficiary. And at the same time, it permits the property to qualify under the marital deduction rule. Here is an illustration:

Tony Robbins, an affluent fellow, provides in his will that his surviving spouse will have a life estate in the small four-unit apartment building he owns. Thus, his widow is permitted to use one of the apartments during her lifetime and receive all rental income from the property. She is given no other interest in the property. Consequently, she has no right to sell the building or to designate a beneficiary to inherit it when she dies. When she dies, the building is inherited by Robbins's oldest daughter, one of his three adult children, as specified in his will.

Something else happened when Robbins's widow was granted the life estate to the apartment building: Robbins's executor filled out a tax form arranging to have the property treated as a marital deduction. Remember that this is allowed under the new tax law even though the widow is not given the right to name the ultimate beneficiary of the property. The tax is not due when Robbins, the grantor, dies. However, it is computed at the time of the widow's death. This, then, is what the new law calls a qualified terminable interest.

Thus, the effect of the rules surrounding the qualified terminable interest is twofold:

• First, the final disposition of the property can be decided by the grantor (in this case, Robbins). He or she can name the ultimate beneficiary of the property following the death of his or her spouse. At the same time, the property still will qualify as a marital deduction in the estate of the first spouse, meaning that taxes may be postponed for years.

• Second, although the executor of the surviving spouse—after the death of that individual—must pay the estate tax due on the qualified property, the executor can regain the tax from those who are the ultimate beneficiaries of the property. This safeguards the executor's ability to pay other bequests and other taxes.

No doubt the qualified terminable interest will be used frequently. For instance, someone who owns property, fearing that his or her spouse might be capricious or improperly influenced by others, might use this new rule to make certain that specified property would ultimately go to the beneficiaries of his or her choice, or maybe to beneficiaries agreed upon earlier by the couple. Such actions could be taken under past laws but only upon the loss of a tax advantage. Now the tax advantage can be kept.

The new rule should solve some special problems, too. An example concerns the owner of property who has a second wife or husband. That individual could give his or her second spouse a life estate in the property and, at the same time, assure that it won't be shifted away from the intended beneficiaries—possibly the children of the grantor's first marriage.

Jointly Held Property

Under past tax laws, property held jointly by a husband and wife became part of the taxable estate of the spouse who died first. Property was defined not only as real estate but passbook savings accounts, certificates of deposit, common stocks, and most other items of value. Certain exceptions were made to this rule, but they were rare. The Internal Revenue Service, for example, considered only such cases involving surviving spouses who could prove that they had bought the property in question with their money, not with the earnings of their spouse. The same was true of savings accounts and savings certificates: Surviving spouses were required to show to the IRS's satisfaction that the money in question belonged to them—for it to be nontaxable in the decedent's estate.

Under the Economic Recovery Tax Act, all of this is abolished. Beginning in 1982, jointly owned property is treated in a set manner regardless of which spouse bought or paid for it or whose money rests in joint accounts. Under the new law, when one spouse dies, one-half of the value of the jointly held property becomes part of the estate of the deceased spouse. The surviving spouse retains ownership of the other half. No exceptions are made.

This change in the tax law appears logical: Marriage is a partnership. Joint assets should be treated by the Internal Revenue Service as such. The change also seems harmless. It is, but only to a point. Here is an example of *income tax* problems the new rule can create:

In 1970, Todd and Pam Mays purchased a home for $60,000 and listed the property in both names. The money used to buy the house was provided by Todd, an electrician. Pam did not contribute to it: She was a full-time homemaker. In January of 1982, Todd died suddenly of a heart attack. By this time, the couple's home had appreciated in value to $130,000. Under the new law, half of this amount becomes part of Todd's estate.

The problem here is not with estate taxes—Pam owes nothing to the government, since the house qualifies under the unlimited marital deduction provided in the new law. Rather, the difficulty comes when she decides to sell the house.

Under past law, Pam would pay no taxes on the sale if she received the appraised value of the property—$130,000. This was because, in the IRS's view, she did not realize a profit on the sale of the house. She inherited a home from her husband valued at $130,000 and sold it for $130,000. She received no taxable gain.

Under the new law, this scenario is altered. Pam still sells the home for $130,000, but now the Internal Revenue Service determines that she has made a profit and, consequently, a tax is due. This is why:

Pam retains ownership of one-half of the house. She inherits the other half. Under the new law, the value of the house for tax purposes (a figure referred to as the "tax basis") is computed by adding (1) the value of the surviving spouse's 50 percent share of the property and (2) one-half of its original cost. In this instance, the total is $95,000, the sum of $65,000 (the value of Pam's half of the house) plus $30,000 (half of the original purchase price). When the house is sold, a tax is due on the difference between the selling price and the "tax basis"—$130,000 minus $95,000, or $35,000. The tax is figured at the capital gains rate, which is computed individually by multiplying 40 percent by the profit by the taxpayer's marginal tax bracket. (See chapter 8.)

True, the capital gains tax rate *is* lower than what we pay on normal earnings. Yet that is not of much help in sweetening the situation. Under the previous law, *no* tax would be due. Thus, the new estate rules on joint ownership can lead to income tax problems that did not exist before.

Lifetime Giving

Among the more dramatic changes mandated by the Economic Recovery Tax Act are the rules governing gifts made by the living. Until 1982, each of us was permitted to give up to $3,000 tax-free each year to each of our children or other donees, meaning they were not required to pay any sort of tax on the amounts they received. If our spouses joined in this giving, the amount we were allowed to distribute to our off-springs rose to $6,000 each. This meant that a couple with three children could make tax-free gifts of $18,000 a year. One reason for doing this, of course, was to avoid taxes. By distributing a portion of our assets, we could decrease the size of our estate and thereby decrease the estate taxes due at the time of our deaths. For example, the couple mentioned previously could cut the value of their estate by $180,000 if they gave their children the maximum allowed over a 10-year period.

The new tax law not only keeps intact such mechanisms for distributing assets but enhances them. It accomplishes this by increasing the maximum annual amount we may give each of our children or other donee to $10,000 (if the gift is made by one spouse) or $20,000 (if it is made by both spouses). A couple with three children, then, could remove from their estates as much as $600,000 over 10 years. The benefit of this is easy to understand. Consider this example:

Dr. Benjamin Fields has assets totaling $2.4 million. During the 10 years beginning in 1982, he and his wife join in making annual gifts to their three children up to the maximum tax-free amount—$600,000. Dr. Field then dies, leaving half of the original $2.4 million, or $1.2 million to his wife, and the remaining $600,000 to the children. His widow, because of the marital deduction, pays no taxes on the portion of the estate she receives. The children pay no taxes either, because the amount they inherit is within the $600,000 provided in the new tax law. Dr. Fields's plan works: By distributing a substantial part of the value of his property prior to his death, he carries out his objective in dividing his wealth—and his heirs avoid paying estate taxes.

The point here, at least for those having sizable assets, is that lifetime gift planning is a valuable tool for keeping taxable estates below the $600,000 taxation breaking-point.

One catch to gift giving under past tax laws was a regulation known as the "three-year rule." What this did was penalize the family of an individual who made gifts to the family within three years of his death. The IRS, under established law, viewed such gifts as made "in contemplation of death"— meaning they were assumed to have been made deliberately to avoid taxation. Thus, the gifts became part of the taxable estate. Since few of us know when we are going to die, the three-year rule rankled many professional estate planners and their clients.

The authors of the Economic Recovery Tax Act apparently agreed. Under the new law, the three-year rule is ignored. Gifts—apart from the transfer of ownership of insurance policies—are excluded from the estate of the person making them, regardless of the timing. A gift could be made a month or a year or 10 years before the death of the donor. It will make no difference. The gift still will not be part of the decedent's estate.

The Effects of the New Tax Law

The impact on individuals of all these changes in gift and estate taxes under the new 1981 tax law is substantial. It is far-reaching. Some groups, in particular, will benefit. Specifically:

• Business executives, professionals, scientists, high-salaried engineers, successful sales people, persons who hold inherited wealth, and the owners of farms and small businesses now will be able to pass along more of their money and assets to their heirs knowing they will not have to pay substantial taxes.

After all, the old law that existed as late as 1976 which permitted a tax-free inheritance of a mere $60,000 was unreasonable. Even the 1981 tax-free inheritance cap of $176,000 was not high enough, given the distortion of the dollar by double-digit inflation (including zooming real estate prices). By 1981 that $176,000 exclusion (legislated in 1976) was worth only $110,000 in true dollar value. Obviously, the amount individuals were allowed to receive free of estate taxation needed to be raised—and it was.

• Much of the pressure to raise money for inheritance taxes will be removed from small-business and farm owners.

The price of quality farm acreage rose nearly 250 percent between 1970 and 1981. (Indeed, a prime-quality 500-acre farm in the Kansas wheat fields today carries a price tag of as much as $1.5 million.) The price of a suburban store building near a major city rose 150 percent in prime locations in the 1970s. Where, in tax terms, did these inflated values leave those who inherited farms or small businesses? The answer is, In bad shape. For example, in 1980 a family inheriting a taxable estate of $1 million—in liquid investments, a farm, or small business—paid well over $300,000 in federal estate taxes.

Here are three examples of what this means:

• You owned a large building-supply store. Your building itself was worth $200,000, and the stock $200,000 (a reasonable figure for such merchandise). You died in 1981. Your family wanted to continue the business but faced an estate tax bill of, say, $50,000, an amount they found very difficult to pay. They learned that a forced sale of merchandise could be punishing. This example is realistic. Such hardships have been common. The new law helps greatly in most such cases.

• You own 50 percent of a wholesale paint business, and your partner holds the other half. You die suddenly. Previously high estate taxes might have meant that your family would be forced to sell your half of the business, or possibly just half of your share, to raise estate tax money. But selling under forced conditions brings a low price—and you may have neglected to anticipate this by means of an agreement with your partner. If your family sells only part of your share of the business, say 25 percent of the whole business, they are left with a minority interest, and this may mean no voice or control over operations.

• Your family has been farming the 300 acres that you have owned for over 30 years. You die, leaving the farm to your two sons. Under previous tax laws, your sons might well have needed to sell off, say, 150 acres to satisfy the demands of the IRS. This could have destroyed the economic viability of the farm. For instance, it could have meant not being able to diversify or rotate crops as required, or not being able to buy supplies as cheaply or rent expensive harvesting or other farm equipment.

For many owners of small businesses and professionally run farms, the new law means that using costly insurance to protect against estate tax emergencies will no longer be necessary. It has been customary for many small business people and farmers to pay several thousand dollars a year in life insurance premiums for policies covering the owner's life. Death taxes have been the biggest motivation.

Now, for example, an estate of $1 million can be fully protected under the new law. No estate taxes will be owed if the owner leaves a large part of the property to his spouse so that the remainder falls below the taxation level. Starting in 1987, up to $1.2 million can be left "50–50" to your spouse and children, tax-free, with $600,000 going to each. By proper use of trusts—which require specific advice—estate taxes may be avoided as of the time of the husband's death (assuming he dies first) and at the time of the wife's death as well, with the principal of the estate going to the children to be taxed at some distant future time. These arrangements are complex, however, and are only suitable in certain family situations. A qualified estate lawyer should be consulted.

• There will be more emphasis on saving for the next generation now that more of what we own will be safe from the Internal Revenue Service.

It is quite true that many couples in their fifties and sixties—the more prosperous of those, that is—have for years believed that it is better to spend than leave it behind for the U.S. Treasury. If we don't benefit from our money, the government will, they have said. Under the new law, a considerably larger share of an individual's wealth will go to his legatees, not to the government.

Along with this greater emphasis on saving for "the kids," in some families there will be *less* emphasis on taking large sums of money out of one's potential taxable estate while one is still alive. The popular strategy of "assigning" ownership of a large life insurance policy to one's spouse no longer has the appeal it once had. Also, despite the liberal new rules on gifts made during one's lifetime, some people, at least, may feel that lifetime gifts as a means of removing wealth from the estate are not necessary. Once again, the complexities of estate planning suggest that you check with an advisor.

You and Your Will

Review your will *if* you have one. If you don't have a will, make one. These sound like old saws. They are, but they are important, given the number of changes made in estate and gift taxation under the Economic Recovery Tax Act. Also, keep these points in mind:

• *Don't make the mistake of assuming that the value of your estate will fall below the tax-free ceilings established by the federal government.* If you are employed by a company providing a full range of insurance and other retirement benefits, if you are a professional or a manager in a well-paying job, there is a good chance that the value of your estate will be well beyond $600,000 in the next 5, 10, or 15 years. Assess your net worth realistically and regularly. Make no assumptions. If you do, your heirs may pay for it.

• *Don't overlook "hidden" assets.* Many corporate executives are cash poor—that is, they have little saved and spend most of their annual salaries and bonuses. They tend to overlook the dollar values accumulating in their corporate fringe benefit package—especially under company group insurance plans. These often contribute triple an executive's final salary, sometimes more, to the estate. These values should not be ignored when assessing your net worth.

• *Consider inflation in your estate planning.* This is more difficult, but the impact of inflation should be weighed, particularly its effect on the amount you leave for the care of a dependent—a handicapped child, for example.

• *Don't abandon the notion of setting up trust funds.* You may want to safeguard children or possibly aging parents. If you do, trusts remain among the better vehicles available. A lawyer will be required, though, and that will mean a fee of $500 to $1,000 or more. You and your spouse, if you are married, also may need to write tandem wills to include the establishment of a trust or trusts.

• *Finally, remember that the key in estate management is the same as in financial management—sound, thorough planning.* And the new 1981 tax law makes all of this more pertinent.

Chapter 11 _____

Supplement: What the New Tax Law Does for Small Business

You have owned a family business for many years. You have worked 12-hour days, time and again, to make things hum. And you have worked Saturdays and Sundays at times, to make Monday mornings run smoothly. Your antique shop, or men's store, or lumberyard, or movie house, or machine tool shop, or consulting business, or accounting firm, whatever it is—has been a lifetime work, and a lifelong friend.

The business has been profitable but not really a gold mine, and increasingly in recent years, the problems of inflation and high interest costs have taken their toll. More and more, some form of help on the financial front—even help from the government, maybe in the shape of lower taxes—began to seem like a good idea. At least, you could hope for such a break—and why *not* a tax break? Heaven knows, you had *paid* enough over the years to the IRS.

And over the past two years, in fact, beginning about in January of 1980, your attention was drawn to the "tax talk" that began flooding out of Washington, D.C., in a torrent of words and promises. The politicians and the small business organizations in the nation's capital made promises galore:

As a small business owner, you would enjoy sizable small-business corporate tax cuts.

As a small business owner, you would receive some amazing tax breaks in the form of fast tax depreciation rules for your investments in equipment and real estate.

As a small-business owner, you would gain a great advantage because the estate tax laws were going to be radically revised—so that people who owned small businesses would not have to sell out, or sell out in part, to pay the U.S. Treasury its huge estate and gift taxes.

So much for promises. As it turned out, the tax help came in bunches—but not too much of it was designed to help small business in special ways. The one great bonanza for the "smalls"—the one promise to pan out beautifully—was the revision of the estate tax laws. *That* one came through (see chapter 10). The other items on the promise list turned out to be disappointing. Not only were the tax cuts for small corporations less than promised—much less—but the depreciation deduction rules, as it worked out, were designed very heavily in favor of the big companies. *They* were the ones that invested in the fast-write-off industrial equipment in big amounts, and in plants and factories—not the little business with its delivery truck or two and its small quarters (probably leased from a landlord who would get the advantage of the faster depreciation).

So, as it turned out, the Economic Recovery Tax Act of 1981 isn't really a "recovery act" at all—if you own one of the millions of small businesses that gross under $500,000 or $600,000, or so.

The Corporate Rate Cuts and the "Fast Write-Off" Rules

There are more changes, but two provisions in the new law have the widest impact on small business: tax cuts and depreciation write-off rules.

The rate cuts are anything but monumental: The corporate rates for the lowest two $25,000 tax brackets (that is, up to

$50,000 of taxable income) go down one percent for tax years beginning in 1982, and another one percent for 1983. The tax tables for small corporations are shown in figure 11–1.

FIGURE 11–1

| | TAX | | |
Taxable Income	1981	1982	1983
Income	(old law)		(and later)
up to $25,000	17%	16%	15%
25,000–50,000	20	19	18
50,000–75,000	30	30	30
75,000–100,000	40	40	40
100,000 and up	46	46	46

Not only were no rate cuts made covering the crucial $50,000 to $100,000 range (as had been expected), but the cash savings in the lowest brackets turned out to be pitiably small:

• A company with a taxable income of $25,000 paid $4,250 in corporate taxes for 1981, and—under the new law—will pay $3,750 for 1983 and later years. Saving: $500 a year.

• With a taxable income of $50,000, the 1981 tax was $9,250 ($25,000 at 17 percent plus $25,000 at 20 percent), and the 1983 tax is $8,250 (same formula). Saving: $1,000 a year.

• For corporations in the $50,000 to $100,000 taxable income range there is *no* change in the tax rates and no saving, and at $100,000 and up, a small company is on a par with the big international corporations, with a tax rate of 46 percent.

Secondly, the new law provides businesses of all sizes with faster depreciation schedules, enabling a company to write off via tax deductions the cost of new equipment and buildings over a much shorter span of years than under the old law. The effect is to increase cash flow, especially in the early years of ownership. The new Accelerated Cost Recovery System (ACRS) replaces the old law's Asset Depreciation Range (ADR) system by which write-offs were based on the "useful life" of the equipment or commercial real estate, and which involved far longer time periods.

The new ACRS idea is that a company gets back the money it invested sooner, and thus is able to buy new equipment or buildings sooner, and thus thwart—or tend to thwart— the effects of inflation. The sooner a company buys, the better off it is in terms of avoiding higher prices. The write-off periods are as follows:

- 15 years: business, commercial, and industrial real estate.
- 10 years: certain public utility property.
- 5 years: machinery and equipment.
- 3 years: autos and lightweight trucks, research and development (R&D) equipment, and special tools that wear out rapidly.

Generally, these new tax write-offs are available as of January 1, 1981. This means that if your business made investments in equipment or real estate since that date, you should review with a tax accountant the possibility that your company may be entitled to refunds of prior taxes paid. Thus, the advantages of the faster write-offs can be great for a small business— to the extent that the business makes capital investments. This point, however, is the rub, since it is true that about 85 percent of all small businesses are labor-intensive, *not* capital-intensive—especially in retail lines, service lines, and in the construction field. If your primary investment is in the people you hire—instead of the equipment and buildings you buy—you gain little from this section of the new tax law.

This is not to say that the new law provides only crumbs for most small enterprises. Some new tax benefits are clear. For example, if a small business in a retail line buys a store building for, say, $150,000, there is an advantage in the fast 15-year depreciation of the building—possibly not a great advantage, but meaningful. Under the old law, the building usually would have been written off in about 35 years—at the rate of some $4,300 a year in depreciation tax deductions. The new law's 15-year write-off on a straight-line basis—that is, deducting the same amount for 15 years, which usually is most advantageous—permits a tax deduction each year of $10,000. This is an obvious advantage.

However, the question is, *How much* will the tax deduction be worth to the business? If a larger company is in the 46 percent tax bracket, each dollar of tax deduction saves the company 46 cents. If a small business, however, is in the 19 percent bracket in 1982—the saving is 19 cents on the dollar. In fact, some leading tax accountants who specialize in small business taxation, have been trying of late to impress clients with the need to analyze their company taxes in this manner.

One example cited is that of the owner of a small business who in 1982 bought a new high-speed press to be used in his print shop. The press cost $10,000. Under the old law (ADR method), the first-year tax write-off on the press would have been $3,600. The new ACRS write-off comes to $7,000 (using the new special rules permitting equipment to be depreciated in five years and on an accelerated year-to-year schedule). However, this owner's business falls in the lowest corporate tax bracket for 1982, since its taxable income will range from about $23,000 to $24,000. On this level, the new law dropped the tax rate only one point: from 17 percent in 1981 to 16 percent in 1982 (with another 1 point drop in 1983). This means that the business will save only a small amount of money on the modest change in the tax rate—the business might save $500 at most. In addition, the business will save only 16 cents on each dollar of tax deduction.

Thus, the owner of such a business, say the specialists, has little tax motivation to invest in new equipment. The point is that the new law—by providing higher tax deductions as its principal form of tax relief to business—rewards those companies most that are in the maximum 46 percent corporate tax bracket. For them, a dollar of depreciation deduction saves 46 cents—but not so for a small business paying at far lower rates. A tax credit—an amount taken "off the top" of the final tax owed the government—would have better served the smalls.

In the above print shop example, $7,000 or the $10,000 cost of the high-speed press can be written off in the first year, using the new ACRS five-year depreciation formula. The cash saving, as against a $3,600 write-off under the old rules, comes to $544: 16 percent (the tax bracket) times $3,400 (the additional amount deducted). As it happened, in the print shop case, the owner invested savings in the machine. However, if the company had borrowed the $10,000 to buy the equipment—which is the more usual situation—it probably would have paid at least 18 percent in interest. Its interest cost for the first year of the loan would have been $1,800. Thus, under the new tax law, the $544 saving would amount to only 30 percent of the cost of the equipment loan.

Bigger companies are crunched by high interest rates, of course—but, for them, the more valuable tax write-offs ease the punishment.

Adding insult to injury: The new tax law does not provide equal tax depreciation advantages, industry to industry. For example, office buildings, on average, were written off via depreciation deductions over 41 years, using the old ADR method. The deductions were small, year-to-year. Under the new law, the timing is 15 years and the depreciation tax deductions—as illustrated in the print shop case—are much bigger. Thus, for office buildings, the reduction in the write-off time is 63 percent. For apartment buildings, the reduction in write-off time is 53 percent—an advantage, but not quite so great. But small business, once again, misses out in the size of the tax advantages provided:

• The reduction in tax write-off time for office furniture and fixtures—major items in many small businesses—is only 37 percent. It is the difference between an average 8-year write-off under the old law, and five years under the new law.

Probably the writers of the new tax law found the change unavoidable; still the change fails to provide a great many small businesses with a maximum tax advantage.

• The write-off treatment of autos and light trucks—mainstay items for several million small retail and service businesses—is possibly the biggest put-down of a group found in the new tax law. Autos and light trucks, on average, were written off under the old law in three years—*and* are under the new law in three years, as well. *No* write-off advantage is provided, and, moreover, the old tax credit for the purchase of business autos and light trucks was raised from a low 3.3 percent to only 6 percent—whereas the standard investment tax credit for equipment is 10 percent. Some small business groups have complained of such disparities, but thus far to no avail.

The Curtailed Equipment Allowance

Under the old law, a capital investment "expense allowance" provided the smallest businesses with a minor tax break. They could deduct as a business expense 100 percent of the cost of an item of equipment, and not worry about spreading out the recapture of the cost using depreciation deductions over several years. They could take the deduction in one bite, and thus improve cash flow. The only catch was that the limit of this annual allowance was a mere $2,000.

In 1980, small business groups in Washington began talking up the idea of extending the expense allowance, and the politicians joined in. The push on behalf of the smalls was for a $25,000-a-year allowance, and it was recognized that if the average small company could "expense" (deduct totally in the year of purchase) up to $25,000 in newly bought equipment, the change would materially help 90 percent of all small enterprises. This is easy to understand. If a company in, say, the 18 percent tax bracket, bought a $20,000 truck or factory machine, and could take an expense deduction for the $20,000 in the year of purchase, the tax deduction would save the company 18 cents on the dollar. In effect, the company would have bought the equipment at an 18 percent discount—in this case, for $20,000 minus $3,600, or $16,400.

No such luck for the smalls, however. They must be content with a lesser benefit. Skipping 1981 but starting in 1982, the expense allowance is jumped to $5,000, and it reaches a maximum of $10,000, as shown in figure 11–2.

FIGURE 11–2

Tax Year	Allowance
1981	none
1982	$ 5,000
1983	5,000
1984	7,500
1985	7,500
1986 and later years	10,000

A limitation is that the usual 10 percent investment tax credit available upon the purchase of depreciable equipment is lost if the item bought is "expensed" under the above allowance privilege. This amounts to a built-in watering-down of the allowance advantage. True, if a small business in the 18 percent tax bracket buys a piece of equipment for $1,000, it gets an effective 18 percent discount if it takes a $1,000 expense deduction in the year of purchase. But if the business loses a 10 percent tax credit in the bargain, the full value of the 18 percent discount is cut in half. In short: a limited benefit.

Two more changes in the tax law are specifically "targeted" to help small businesses: an easier rule covering the ban on excessive "accumulated earnings," and a liberalization that benefits "subchapter S" corporations.

• Subchapter S. A corporation that elects subchapter S

status (the name taken from a passage in the tax law) is not taxed as a corporation. Instead, each shareholder of the company pays taxes on his or her share of the corporation's income, using the usual personal tax return filing. There are some strings attached, but generally, the idea works well for many smaller, family-controlled businesses.

The new tax law says simply that beginning in 1982, the number of shareholders in a subchapter S corporation may go as high as 25 persons. The old limit was 15. The idea is to make subchapter S status more practical for more and somewhat larger-size businesses. Another technical easing allows certain trusts (as owners of property and taxpayers) to be shareholders in such a company.

One prime advantage is that the owners of the company maintain "limited liability" as to third persons, as in the case of corporate ownership generally. In some cases, individual shareholders who are in high-income brackets are able to split off or shift income to spouses, children, or other relatives who are in lower tax brackets. This is done by making annual gifts of stock in the company to the family members—and the result can be lower income taxes for the family as a group.

• Accumulated earnings. This liberalization benefits a number of small company owners who build up funds in the company—refraining from paying out profits as dividends. A certain level of accumulation is permitted because it is assumed that any business needs a pool of money for future operations and expansion. Beyond a certain level, however, the assumption is made that the owner is merely keeping the money in the company treasury and safe from the Internal Revenue Service.

The new law—effective January 1, 1981—raises the amount that can be accumulated from $150,000 to $250,000. Amounts in excess of $250,000 are subject to a penalty of 27.5 percent of the first $100,000 improperly accumulated.

The Economic Recovery Tax Act of 1981 has many sections that—if not directly targeted to small businesses—relate closely to them. A review in coming weeks or months of the points discussed here probably will be a necessity for you, given the strains and stresses of owning and operating a small business in difficult times. A tax accountant would be needed, no doubt, and a fee that might range from $40 to $60 an hour to $100 or more an hour, surely will be money well spent. Obviously, one cannot view the new tax law as a panacea for a small business. Yet to ignore it will cost some hard cash, and maybe considerable amounts of it.

Index ———————————————————————

INDEX

INDEX

INDEX